- Small Groups

- Families

- Individuals

by David and Elaine Howlett

Published by WriteLife, LLC
2323 S. 171 St.
Suite 202
Omaha, NE 68130
www.writelife.com

in cooperation with

Grief Illustrated Press
PO Box 4600
Omaha, NE 68104
www.centering.org

Printed in the United States of America

ISBN 978 1 60808 037 3

First Edition

Dedicated to the Glory of God

In loving memory of,

Our precious son, Craig Daniel Howlett;

Nephew, Steven Eugene Shaw;

Nieces, Amanda Lou Shaw and Michelle Lynne Howlett;

Brother, Ronald Dean Shaw

And in honor of,

Our children

Aaron and Catie Howlett;
Bryon Howlett

And grandchildren

Emma and Lucian Howlett

HOW TO USE THIS BOOK

While *"Lazarus, Come Out!"* is basically designed to be used in and best serves small groups, we recognize this is not always possible.

You can make good use of the material here as a family or as an individual searching for a path toward faith.

However you use it, we wish you
gentleness in your journey,
faith in your travels
and comfort in your hearts.

Preface: A Note from Elaine and David

The temperature on June 28, 2000, was hovering around the 100 degree mark accompanied by an oppressively high humidity. It was moving day for United Methodist pastors, and we had relocated from a small town in northern Missouri to another small town in the middle of the state, a distance of about 90 miles. The move gave David the opportunity to minister to a new congregation, and we were looking forward to the challenges that lay ahead.

All of the boxes and furniture were moved in, and the moving van had left. If you've moved before, you know the scene. Boxes were everywhere, and nothing was in its place. We were exhausted from the labor of the day and the weather. We went out to eat dinner, arriving back at our new home around 7:00 o'clock that evening.

We were home about 10 minutes, when we received the phone call that every parent fears. It truly is a parent's worst nightmare. Our youngest son, Craig, had been killed in a car accident.

Instantly, our lives became sheer turmoil and chaos. We couldn't think; we couldn't move; we couldn't breathe. It was as if the world kept moving, and we were not a part of it. Confusion, disbelief, and horror gripped both of us. We became useless to each other, our surviving children, and our God.

We weren't surprised by the severe emotional and mental upheaval or even the intense physical pain, but it was several weeks before we acknowledged the crisis of faith we were experiencing. Our faith took a direct hit. Its foundation was shaken. There were very real and troubling questions that traditional thought or a seminary degree could not answer.

We weren't prepared for any of it. Who could be? Parents don't allow themselves to even think about the possibility, in fear that it will come true. Everyone says, "I can't imagine what you're going through." They are right. We couldn't have imagined it either, much less prepared for it.

We have discovered that, for most people, grief is four-sided. Grief is experienced emotionally, mentally, physically, and spiritually.

We define spiritual grief as mourning our relationship with God.
It may even result in a lost relationship with the Creator.

Throughout this workbook, we refer to God using masculine pronouns. We realize this severely limits God. God is so much more than we can ever hope, dream, and imagine. God is not a greater and bigger version of us. God is God, but it seems our finite human minds benefit from images of God as a person and someone with whom we can build a relationship. The scriptures, especially the Psalms, so eloquently describe God in terms in which we can relate. For instance, "I have engraved you on the palms of my hands," says the Lord (Isaiah 49:14-16).

There are many questions that are common to most grieving parents.

The biggest and most problematic is, **WHY???**

• Why did God take my child?

• At the very least, why did God, the Protector of our children, allow it to happen?

• Many parents feel abandoned by God, disillusioned, and disappointed in God.

• They may even have intense anger with God.

Sometimes, this results in great fear. Anger toward God can be very scary. Without a strong belief in God, purpose in life may be lost. At the very least, there are usually very deep-seated trust issues in a loving God.

Our intent with this study guide is to expose the scriptures in such a way that healing and spiritual growth take place. It may be helpful to purchase or borrow a New International Version of the Bible, as there are some places where you are invited to "fill in the blanks" based on this version. This method forces a focus on key words that we deem important and adds an appreciation to details that might otherwise be missed.

We will not attempt to explain or defend God. However, we will share our faith renewal where we deem it appropriate and helpful. We have spent many hours wrestling with some very hard questions. We believe God has given us some knowledge to share. We don't know why Craig's death happened, nor will we ever know in this life, **WHY???** Yet, we have come to a place of renewed trust in a loving God, honest joy, and a peace that surpasses understanding.

TABLE OF CONTENTS

INTRODUCTION

We spent hours searching for impossible answers to endless questions. Yet, walking away from God and all the questions wasn't an acceptable option for us either. The torment was frustrating and extremely painful.

Coming back to a healthy relationship with God didn't just happen. Overcoming grief or a broken relationship with God took some hard work. In order to get better, we both had to decide that we wanted to trust God fully again. Once the decision was made, then we had to make a commitment to seek God and listen for His voice. God began revealing Himself to us in varied ways and many times quite unexpectedly. He continues to this day to surprise us with bits and pieces of the bigger picture that only God understands. Even though the path was pretty rugged at times, the journey was well worth the effort.

What we have now is not answers to all of the endless questions. Some questions don't have answers and others we won't have answered in this life. Like Job, we are confident that some answers are too wonderful for us to know.

> "I know that you can do all things:
> no plan of yours can be thwarted.
> You asked, 'Who is this that obscures my
> counsel without knowledge?'
> Surely I spoke of things I did not understand,
> things too wonderful for me to know."
> Job 42:2-3 (NIV)

Like Job, we have discovered the true character of God. God is loving and worthy of trust. The Bible reveals all we need to know to believe this is true.

What we hope is that you will seek God and allow the scriptures to open up the Truth to you. You'll need to spend time in prayer and genuine study. We can't give you our relationship with God; however, we can attest that it is worth every effort to take the journey.

While this study can be done individually, we believe the most effective use of it is with a small group (6-12 people). A group of this size will help you learn, provide support to be honest, and help you to continue through the intense moments. Each member of the group will do the daily studies on his/her own and meet once a week with the group to share struggles, insights, and personal faith journey. No one should be asked to share beyond what they are comfortable and ready to share. We believe we are created by God for a relationship with Him. God's desire is that we know how much He loves us. We are praying for you.

Week One

THE FOUR SIDES OF GRIEF

WEEK ONE
THE FOUR SIDES OF GRIEF

Each of us is comprised of mind, body, and spirit. Therefore, our grief is experienced emotionally, physically, mentally, and spiritually. Emotional, mental, and physical grief will be mentioned only briefly and then the rest of this study will focus on spiritual grief.

Words cannot express the depth of sadness, despair, and pure anguish we feel when a child dies. Grief is the price we pay for loving them and the depth of our grief is equal to the depth of our love. Our unconditional love doesn't stop when they die. If anything, it gets stronger. Uncontrollable tears swell from a heart that is sick with unbearable pain. We feel they are worthy of every tear.

Psalm 139 describes the human body as fearfully and wonderfully made (vs. 14). The hormones that carry the message from the brain to the tear ducts to produce tears of sadness are also carrying messages all over the body. Every cell grieves. We ache all over. Our arms and legs feel like lead weights. Some people want to sleep all of the time. Others can't sleep. Some people experience an extreme fight or flight syndrome where one wants to open the door and run without any particular destination in mind. I'm sure you can add to this list some of your own physical symptoms of intense grief. That's normal—for the grieving.

Mentally, we're confused, forgetful, and sometimes worry that we're losing our minds. We think we see our child walking in a crowd. We go into room after room looking for something and cannot remember what it was.

Then there's the spiritual side of grief:

- ☒ Where was God?
- ☒ Where is God now?
- ☒ Is there a God?
- ☒ Was I a fool to believe?

As already mentioned, we define spiritual grief as a broken relationship with God. Our greatest desire for you is a healing of that relationship through prayer and His Word. It's a personal journey you'll need to take. Our intention is not to tell you what to believe. Our intention is to help you discover a foundation for building a rock-solid belief system on which to build your life. Our doctrine or theology may differ from your beliefs. What's important is that you develop a strong and healthy relationship with God so that your life has purpose and meaning.

DAY 1: EMOTIONAL, MENTAL, AND PHYSICAL GRIEF

Open each day's study with this prayer or one of your own:

God of all time,
Of all that is seen and unseen,
In our confusion and darkness let your light shine
That in our dark world of grief we may find you.

Amen

Emotional Grief

It's easy to understand that grief affects our emotions. The depth of sadness and despair is something to which all of us can relate. However difficult it may be, we must honestly acknowledge our emotions for the healing to begin.

1. Name your emotions following the loss of your child.

Some of the emotions you may have described are sadness, sorrow, despair, confusion, fear, anger, and numbness. Has someone said to you, "I can't imagine what you are going through?" They can't. Could you have imagined the torment you felt in those first few weeks? It's almost impossible to describe, isn't it? You're possibly struggling for words beyond sad or despair. It's hard to describe in words, isn't it?

Mental Grief

Maybe the best way to describe our mental state is that we are in a fog. Our minds are overwhelmed by what has happened. Things that used to make sense don't appear to anymore. We may not make good decisions or be able to solve simple problems. Mental anguish clouds our thoughts.

2. Describe changes in your mental thought processing ability as a result of your grief.

Loss of memory, inability to focus, confusion, loss of concentration, or forgetfulness may be some of things you listed. Maybe you felt your mind played tricks on you—like seeing your child in a crowd. Did you think you may even go crazy?

Physical Grief

Physical grief is a by-product of emotional, mental, and spiritual grief. In other words, it's caused by emotional, mental, and spiritual grief. It doesn't stand or exist alone. The physical pain, however, is real and sometimes scary. At times we may feel our body is out of control.

3. Describe the physical symptoms you experienced early in your grief.

Physical grief can be experienced in a variety of ways; aching all over, heaviness of legs and arms, shakiness, insomnia, loss of appetite, heart pounding, mind racing, and restlessness to name a few. For many of us, our hormones become out of balance leading to conditions such as diabetes. This is by no means an exhaustive list but it's a start. The point is that our bodies suffer the pain of grief also.

4. Are you getting better?

If you haven't seen a doctor, you really need to. There are some remedies for some of the symptoms. The prolonged stress that accompanies parental grief needs professional medical attention to prevent long-term and permanent damage to our health. We certainly aren't qualified to give medical advice to each other. Please see a doctor.

Spiritual Grief

From this point to the end of this study, we will be focusing on the spiritual side of grief. We will begin with the Old Testament book of Nehemiah.

Read Nehemiah 1:1—2:3

5. Why was Nehemiah sad?

Nehemiah was one of the many people in exile in Babylon. His homeland, including the city of Jerusalem, was completely conquered by the Babylonians and the once-glorious temple of Solomon was destroyed. He was the King of Persia's cup bearer, which meant that he was the servant who tasted the king's food and drink before giving it to him to insure the king's safety from poisoning.

Nehemiah heard of the terrible conditions of the people and the city from a person who had just returned from Jerusalem. He was deeply saddened by the news of the dismal state of God's city.

One day while Nehemiah was doing his work, the king noticed his appearance and asked what was wrong. Nehemiah took this opportunity to tell the king, "The city where my fathers are buried lies in ruins and its gates have been destroyed by fire." Nehemiah was mourning the loss of his homeland. His grief was spiritual in that his people couldn't properly worship God in the temple and observe other religious practices. He felt separated from God and proper worship. He longed to return to his homeland and the ability to practice the things that bring him close to God.

6. Do you feel as close to God as you did before your child died? Has your faith in God changed? Are you angry with God? Are you disillusioned, confused, or disappointed in God? Are you grieving spiritually?

Our journey through grief to healing is a process that takes time. It requires work! The process often benefits from the help of an outsider—a trusted friend, support group, family, pastor, or professional counselor. If at any time you feel overwhelmed, talk to someone. We strongly believe that this study is best done in a supportive group. We also strongly believe that spiritual grief will take spiritual discipline in order to get better. Prayer, scripture reading, fellowship with other believers, and listening to God are necessary practices for the journey.

DAY 2: SPIRITUAL GRIEF

Opening Prayer:

God of all time,
Of all that is seen and unseen,
In our confusion and darkness let your light shine
That in our dark world of grief we may find you.

Amen

Spiritual grief doesn't exist on its own. It is intertwined with the emotional, mental, and physical sides of grief. Remember that spiritual grief is grieving the relationship we had with God before our child died.

1. What questions of faith have you experienced?

2. How has your image of God changed following the death of your child? If it has changed, how has it changed?

3. Is God a loving God? Do you believe He loves you?

4. Do you trust God?

5. Do you feel you worship God fully? Is it hard to sing praise songs from the heart?

Read Psalm 27: 4-9

6. What is you heart's response to the reading of this Psalm?

These are difficult questions. Please be honest with your answers. If the answers are too intense or difficult to answer right now, that's OK. You can come back later. However, we ask that you don't quit. As already stated, grief is a process requiring work to get better. If you become overwhelmed, skip that question. We encourage you to go to the group session even if you haven't completed the homework. You aren't alone. It is very common to have doubts and questions. It is even very common to have anger against God. We believe it is healthy for you to freely express your doubts and fears. However, it's not healthy to stay in a doubtful, confused, or angry state of mind. That's where the work comes in. Spiritual battles of the heart and mind need spiritual weapons. Spend time in prayer and meditation. We hope this journey through the Bible will be used as a guide. Venture out on your own as God guides you. We also believe that it is vital that you fellowship with other believers. There may be a time when you need their strength of faith. There may be a time when they need yours.

7. Maybe you have found your faith to be a source of comfort and haven't had doubts or fears. If so, has your faith strengthened during the grieving process? Describe.

8. What were the helpful things people said to you concerning faith issues?

9. Would you like to feel closer to God?

10. How do you think your relationship could be improved?

We cannot stress enough that spiritual grief, like all grief, requires work to heal. We prayed when we weren't sure that God was listening. We read our Bible with fear and confusion in our hearts and tears streaming down our faces. We surrounded ourselves with people of faith even when they didn't understand. It's painful. It was difficult but worth the effort to find hope again.

DAY 3: KING DAVID

Opening Prayer:

God of all time,
Of all that is seen and unseen,
In our confusion and darkness let your light shine
That in our dark world of grief we may find you.

Amen

Read 2 Samuel 18:31-19:8

1. What was King David's response to his son, Absalom's, death?

At the time of Absalom's death, he was in full rebellion against his father, King David. In fact, Absalom was plotting to kill him and assume his kingdom. Yet, when word reached the king concerning his son's fate, David was inconsolable. He repeated his son's name and at first refused to acknowledge the efforts and victory of his troops.

2. Even though Absalom was in full rebellion against his father, describe King David's love for his son.

Many parents understand unconditional love differently after the birth of their child. There is nothing a child can do to separate himself from the love of a parent. Right?

3. How did the love that King David had for Absalom affect the relationships with those closest to him?

[King David's general, Joab, was furious with his commander] He said, "Today you have humiliated all your men, who have just saved your life… and the lives of your wives and concubines. You love those who hate you and hate those who love you… You have made it clear today that the commanders and their men mean nothing to you. I see that you would be pleased if Absalom were alive today and all of us were dead." (19:5-6)

4. How do you relate to the story?

Read 2 Samuel 11:1-12:24

5. Notice that we have backed up to a previous story in King David's life. What was David's response to his infant child's illness? (12:15-17)

David pleaded with God for the child. He fasted and went into his house and spent the nights lying on the ground. The elders of his household stood beside him to get him up from the ground, but he refused, and he would not eat any food with them. (12:16-17)

6. In verse 18, the child dies on the seventh day. What was the reaction of the palace servants following the death of the child?

In a word—FEAR. They said, "While the child was still living we spoke to David but he would not listen to us. How can we tell him the child is dead? He may do something desperate."

7. What was David's response following the death of the child? (12:20-25)

David got up from the ground. After he had washed, put on lotions and changed his clothes, he went into the house of the LORD and worshipped. Then he went to his own house and at his request they served him food and he ate.

His servants asked him, "Why are you acting this way? While the child was alive, you fasted and wept, but now that the child is dead, you get up and eat!"

He answered, "While the child was still alive, I fasted and wept. I thought, 'Who knows? The LORD may be gracious to me and let the child live. But now that he is dead, why should I fast? Can I bring him back again? I will go to him, but he will not return to me.'

Then David comforted his wife Bathsheba, and he went to her and lay with her. She gave birth to a son, and they named him Solomon. The LORD loved him, and because the LORD loved him, he sent word through Nathan the prophet to name him Jedidiah.

8. How do you relate to this story?

9. What is your reaction to how you see God in this story?

This is one of the "troubling" stories in the Bible. Clearly, King David understood that God chose to not let his child live because of his sinfulness. We get into trouble by placing our situation in the story. We start speculating that God is dealing with us similarly. We can't do this! Only God knows David's heart and the reasons why He dealt with David's sin in this manner.

Read Psalm 51

Psalm 51 was written by King David in response to his sinfulness by committing adultery with Bathsheba and then trying to hide it by having her husband murdered. It was his humble prayer for forgiveness and cleansing. It asks for mercy from a God who gives unfailing love. He asks to be washed as you would a filthy garment. King David asks for forgiveness for himself and for the people (Zion).

10. What governmental position did David hold?

He was king. He was also anointed by God to rule over Israel in matters of the kingdom of God. He was responsible to God for the well-being of God's people. As king, David was responsible not just for the political well-being of his subjects but for their spiritual health as well. His leadership, while not without flaws, is still the human example of God's covenant, and is the example of how the Kingdom of God is made known on earth. He knew that everything matters to God. He took his responsibility seriously.

DAY 4: NAOMI

Opening Prayer:

God of all time,
Of all that is seen and unseen,
In our confusion and darkness let your light shine
That in our dark world of grief we may find you.

Amen

Read Ruth 1 & 2

1. What has happened to Naomi? Describe Naomi's view of her present and future.

Naomi, her husband and two sons had left their homeland because of a famine. Both of her sons married women in the new land. Naomi's husband died and then her two sons. With the famine over, she wanted to go back home to Bethlehem, Judah. She asked her daughters-in-law to go with her but later told them that they needed to stay in their own homeland. Ruth wanted to stay with Naomi but Orpah stayed behind. Naomi feels empty and without hope.

But Ruth replied, "Don't urge me to leave you or to turn from you. Where you go I will go and where you stay I will stay. Your people will be my people and your God my God. Where you die I will die, and there I will be buried. May the LORD deal with me, be it ever so severely, if anything but death separates you and me." (1:16-17)

*As a note of instruction, we ask that you fill in the blanks from the verse of scripture indicated here and in following passages throughout this workbook where blanks are provided. We believe this method forces a focus on key words that we deem important and adds an appreciation to details that might otherwise be missed.

Verse 20 (NIV) Please fill in the blanks:

"Don't call me Naomi," she told them. "Call me _____, because the Almighty has made my

life _____ _____. I went away _____, but the LORD has brought me back

_____. Why call me Naomi? The LORD has afflicted me, the Almighty has brought misfortune upon me."

In the ancient Near East, a person's name was often descriptive. Naomi's choice of name and her explanation for it are very telling of her sense of desolation—even her God was against her.

2. How do you relate to the story so far?

To fast-forward through the story, Ruth meets and marries Boaz (a relative of Naomi's).

Read Ruth 4:13-17

The Lord enabled Ruth to conceive and she bore a son.

Verses 14-17 (NIV) Please fill in the blanks:

The women said to Naomi: "Praise be to the LORD, who this day has not left you without a _____

_____. May he become famous throughout Israel! He will _____ your life and sustain

you in your old age. For your daughter-in-law who loves you and is better to you than seven sons, has given him birth.

Then, Naomi took the child, _____ _____ in her _____ and _____for

him. The women living there said, "Naomi _____ a _____." And they named him Obed.

He was the father of Jesse, the father of David.

3. Where is God in this story?

In ancient biblical times widowed women without surviving male children were in a difficult situation. More often than not they had no one to provide for them and the future was in fact hopeless with no real options or alternatives. Many women felt that life lost all meaning and purpose. In Naomi's case, she was far from her people and old in age. She even felt abandoned by her God.

Boaz, her kinsman redeemer, bought the land of her husband and took her and Ruth as his responsibility to provide for them. The book of Ruth is primarily a story of Naomi's transformation from despair and apparent hopelessness to happiness and redemption through the selfless, God-blessed acts of Ruth and Boaz.

DAY 5: JOB

Opening Prayer:

God of all time,
Of all that is seen and unseen,
In our confusion and darkness let your light shine
That in our dark world of grief we may find you.

Amen

The Book of Job was difficult to understand before we lost Craig. Maybe because we didn't struggle with it before but rather avoided the hard issues of faith it conjures up. We didn't have a reason to try to understand it. When other grieving parents found out that David was a pastor, they would ask, "What about the Book of Job?" We've spent years wrestling with the book enough to have found comfort there. All of us feel we can relate to Job's suffering.

Read Job 17: 11-15

Verse 17: 11 (NIV) Please fill in the blanks:

My days have passed, _____ _____ _____ _____,

and so are the desires of my heart.

Verse 17: 15 (NIV) Please fill in the blanks:

Where then is my _____ who can see any_____ for me?

Job had lost hope. His plans for the future have been shattered. Shattered dreams are not easily pieced back together. It's difficult to reconstruct a life without our lost child. In the beginning, it's not even something we want to do. We question how we can possibly survive in so much pain.

Read Job 6: 2, 3

These verses describe the heaviness of heart as well as the physical heaviness we felt in the beginning of our grief journey.

Verse 3: 26 (NIV) Please fill in the blanks:

I have no _____, no _____ I have no _____, but only

_____.

Job doesn't want to live. He longs for death to quiet his bitter soul. He describes his state of being as turmoil.

1. How do you relate to these verses from Job?

Job is a book of poetry. As with most poetry, it uses words to paint the picture of intense suffering. Job describes in detail the severe emotional, mental, physical, and spiritual pain of grief.

Yet, Job does not leave us in hopelessness. The book ends with redemption. His redemption was not only of his wealth, health, and family but also of his soul.

We will come back to Job later in our study. For now, don't despair with this brief introduction to probably the most troubling story in the Bible for a grieving parent.

2. What do the stories of King David, Naomi, and Job have in common?

All three are parents who have lost children. All of them blame God for their suffering. All of them questioned God's provision and care for them. All of them grieved spiritually. All of them experienced redemption.

3. How is redemption present in each of these stories?

Read 2 Samuel 23: 5 (King David)

"Is not my house right with God?
Has he not made with me an
everlasting covenant,
arranged and secured in every part"

Read 2 Samuel 12: 24 (King David)

Following the death of King David and Bathsheba's infant son, they had a son—Solomon. Because God loved him, he sent word through Nathan to name him Jedidiah. King David would have understood that the giving of this name suggested that God's special favor rested on Solomon from his birth, and since the name also contained an echo of David's name, it provided assurance to David that God also loved him and would continue his dynasty.[1] David's redemption came through his humility and the acceptance of God's grace.

Read 2 Chronicles 1: 1

God was with Solomon and made him *exceedingly* great. David's dynasty was fulfilled through his son.

Read Ruth 2: 1, 4: 1-22 (Naomi's redemption)

Boaz was a relative of Naomi. When he agreed to take Ruth as his wife, Boaz became Naomi's kinsman-redeemer.

Verse 4: 14 (NIV)

The women said to Naomi: "Praise be to the LORD, who this day has not left you without a kinsman-redeemer." Through Ruth, aged Naomi, has an heir in place of her son, Mahlon. Ruth is included in a new family structure and hope is restored to Naomi. She has a son (verse 16).

Read Job 19: 25

As Christians we celebrate redemption from guilt and sin. In this case, the Redeemer seems to be God himself. Job expresses confidence that ultimately God will vindicate him in the face of the false accusations of his friends. In the end, God will stand to vindicate him.[2] He knows in his heart that one day he will stand before his Redeemer and the

---

[1]NIV text note page 422; NIV Study Bible, Copyright 1985, 1995, 2002 by the Zondervan Corporation
[2]Ibid, page 751

accusations made by his friends will be verified by God as false. Job remained faithful and was relentless in his search to hear from God. In the end, Job does encounter God face to face and was fully restored.

4. The basic meaning of redemption is "deliverance" from the situation in which one is immersed. Is redemption something you seek or desire? Do you resist letting God have a part in your future?

The lesson in these three stories is that in the face of great suffering they remained faithful. Job shook his fist at God and yet didn't denounce Him. He was angry and questioned God's fairness, yet he didn't turn from God. In the end, God restored double all that Satan had taken except his children. He started with ten children and was given ten children. Could it be that the first ten children are with God? We believe so.

Even though we think we can put our situation in each of these stories, God dealt with each person and their story differently. The most important thing we need to see is that God never left them even though they didn't realize he was with them every step of the way. God was at work with a bigger picture in mind and an even more preferred future for them *in their eyes*. Each of them felt they had been restored. We want to interject our own questions and how we think God "should" have acted or responded. In each case, they felt redeemed and right with God.

Terrified of Losing My Faith — by Elaine

I was terrified of losing my faith. Everything I thought was true about God, I questioned. I had prayed at least daily for my children. I especially prayed for their protection and safety. I thought that their safety was a part of God's promises.

As a pastor's wife, I believed (wrongly) that I was entitled to an extra measure of favor from God. After all, as a family, we make huge sacrifices to be in ministry. A United Methodist pastor is appointed. We don't choose where we live. I very much had a "God owes me" attitude.

Then Craig died. What happened? I felt God had abandoned me. How did I fall out of His favor? What did I do wrong, or what had I not done right? Was I a fool to believe in the promises of God? Was I a fool to believe in God at all? What good was faith if it couldn't protect my son?

I could relate to the desolation, despair, and fear that Naomi must have felt.

Every time I closed my eyes, I saw a dark, deep, black hole. I would circle the hole and my feet would slip and slide around it. I knew I was in grave danger of falling into that hole and being lost forever. I thought I was going crazy. What terrified me the most is that without the God I thought I knew, my life had no purpose or meaning and Craig was not in a place called Heaven. He was gone forever and I'd never see him again. I knew I couldn't fake it. God knows my heart.

It was sheer torment. I felt so alone. I felt like damaged goods; like a fraud. David missed one Sunday and he was back in the pulpit preaching. I felt it was my duty to go to church to support him. It took all the courage and strength I could muster to go but it saved my life. I was forced to face my doubts and fears.

Singing the hymns was the hardest and yet they ministered to me profoundly. David chose "Only Trust Him" as one of the hymns shortly after Craig died—within a month or two. *Only trust Him, only trust Him, He will save you now*, are the words that struck such an overwhelming response from my soul. "I trusted You and You didn't save Craig. My son!" I cried as the tears poured down my face. I was so overcome with grief that I slipped out of the sanctuary and fled to David's office. I let God have it. All that had been bottled up for weeks. The tears were hot by now.

"I trusted You and look what happened! You didn't save Craig. How could You take my son," my heart screamed.

To which God replied, "So Craig isn't safe? He's with me you know. You can't trust me with Craig?"

I said, "You know what I mean. He died. He's not safe with me."

God said, "Yes, and you know what I mean. Craig is safe."

It was little comfort at the time but I knew deep down that Craig was with God. It will never be what I want. I will always really, really wish Craig hadn't died, but it was the beginning of a very long and painful journey back to a strong relationship with a God I know loves me and whom I can trust.

Spiritual battles need spiritual weapons for combat. I went to church even though my heart wasn't in it at first. I'm certain others knew because they told me so. I didn't meet their expectations of "pastor's wife", but I did the best I could. There were people who supported us also. I had a close friend whom I met through The Compassionate Friends (TCF). She helped me sort through my feelings about God. TCF is a support group for grieving parents, siblings, and grandparents. The group was extremely helpful for me. There I could be "Elaine" and not "the pastor's wife". They let me talk about Craig all I wanted or needed. They weren't shocked by my feelings toward God.

Like Job, I tried to remain faithful yet honest. I prayed in the midst of confusion. I continued to read my Bible even though I didn't get much out of it at first. Then God began healing the spiritual blindness and I began to see. He began revealing Himself in the Word just for me. You may benefit from my revelation knowledge but wisdom comes directly to the individual. You'll have to do the work too. Through the Holy Spirit, God gave me the understanding I needed. He may speak to you differently or use different scriptures to help you. That's why I think it's best to do this study with a group.

My faith sharing comes in the "for what its worth" category. I'm very certain that God wants a relationship with you and me. I believe that's why we were created. However, my relationship doesn't do you much good—He wants you too. He loves each of us.

I'm so grateful to my God whose love carried me through and wouldn't let me go even when that is what I wanted. He will never leave us or forsake us.

I wrote the following poem on the first anniversary of Craig's death. Like I said, it was the beginning.

God's Rocking Chair

Tossing, turning, tossing, turning
between my burning sheets.
Aching body, breaking heart
tears steaming from the heat.

Confusion, frustration, anger, hate
despair creating a jet black hole.
Pouncing, attacking, tearing, shredding
grief's lion ravaging my soul.

Exhausted, beaten, lonely, raw
I leave my bed for rest.
Bleeding, hurting, tortured, tormented
my child ripped from my breast.

Rocking, rocking, backwards, forwards
empty arms hold your memory.
Rocking, rocking, backwards, forwards
destination…relief from misery.

Aimless, mindless, lifeless, drained
no strength to even pray.
"Help me. Help me. God, help me!"
the only words I can find to say.

Rocking, rocking, whispering, talking
"I'm OK, Mom. I'm safe and warm."
Rocking, rocking, whispering, talking
"I love you, son. You're safe in me."

Rocking, rocking, whispering, talking
"I know, Mom. I love you, too."
Rocking, rocking, whispering, talking
"I miss you, son. I'll never forget you."

Rocking, rocking, whispering, talking
"Goodnight, son." "Goodnight, Mom."
Rocking, rocking, whispering, talking
my child rocks me back to sleep.

Written in loving memory of Craig
July 5, 2001

•••

Driveway Conversations — by David

I call them driveway conversations. They began a few days after Craig's funeral and I, on occasion, still have one. In those first days when the grief was painfully raw, I would go outside as the sun was setting and pace up and down our driveway. I detested sundown. I hated the actual and the symbolic darkness that would begin to surround me. The sun's setting was an indicator that another day had passed without my Craig. As I paced, I would have a conversation with Craig, God, or with myself. Like Elaine, I needed to talk but I also needed kinetic conversation. I couldn't just sit and talk. I needed some physical activity as well.

My conversations were sometimes quiet and other times quite loud. I was always angry. I am sure that our neighbors thought I was a dangerous person. I recall asking Craig where he was. "Are you behind the moon? Are you next to me? Are you even aware of my pain? Can you see me or hear me?" I would ask out loud. I was obsessed with the idea that Craig had to be somewhere. As strange as it sounds now, I wanted to know where heaven was. I knew that Craig was a citizen of heaven; I simply didn't know where heaven was. This knowledge was, at the time, important to me. I thought that knowing would give me a measure of peace. I'm not any more certain today than I was then, but God did send me other sources of comfort to help me get through this season of grief.

The process of recovery started within a day or two of our son's funeral service. Looking back on that period in my

34

life I can see the beginnings of God's care (although, at the time, God's grace didn't seem to be a part of my life at all). However, God's gracious presence began that very week.

God puts people in our lives to encourage us. It is a common phenomenon to lose your lifelong friends after the death of a child. Elaine and I had already left many friends behind by moving to a new setting of ministry the very day of Craig's death. For a few days, we only had ourselves to offer support to each other and then God began to make his presence known to us.

A few days after the funeral, I remembered that I hadn't checked the phone answering machine. There were four messages. I had expected one of the people who left a message to call, but the other three messages were unexpected and helpful to various degrees. Two of those messages still stand out in my memory. One was from a fellow pastor. He and I hadn't been particularly close, and yet his message was simple and sincere. It brought me to tears and comforted me at the same time. The other helpful call was from a funeral director with whom I had worked in my former parish. His message was also unexpected, warm, and compassionate. There would be many more dark days and nights, but the healing had begun.

Within a month of the accident, we attended our first Compassionate Friends (a support group for bereaved parents) meeting. I recall that we were one of three newly bereaved couples at that chapter meeting. Elaine and I made initial contact that night with people who would become powerful allies in our journey through grief.

I began to understand a concept that is still developing. I began to understand that women and men grieve differently. I tried my best to listen to Elaine and she understood my need to walk and talk. It hasn't always been easy, but accepting the differences between how men and women process their hurts and grief has been a God-sent blessing.

I found help in reading. I began to devour books and articles written by people who had lost at least one child. I needed to know that if they could survive then so could I. I was impressed by how so many others honored their children by working with and supporting people like me.

My spiritual life took a major hit with Craig's death. I still believed in God even though that was as much due to not having a viable alternative as real belief. During my evening walks I would talk to God but not in my usual way. I was more like the prophet, Jeremiah. I was angry and hurt. I wanted someone to claim responsibility for this tragedy. I wanted someone to blame. I wanted God to explain why this had happened.

I questioned my faith. I had to participate in a funeral about ten days after my Craig's service. The family knew about my burden so another pastor was asked to help me with the service. I kept asking myself why we were doing any of this at all.

What is the purpose of worship?
Have all my prayers been for nothing?
Did this happen because of some sin I had committed?

I understand now that God listened to my ravings and stayed with me.

God eventually began to give me some direction for my brokenness. I had some powerful encounters with God. I remember waking up on Good Friday of 2001 and before I could get out of bed, God immediately spoke to me with a powerful message. God brought to my memory a verse of scripture that I would never have thought about in such a manner and then gave me an understanding of what the scripture meant for me in my journey. The verse was from 1 Corinthians 13:12. The verse says that now we see but a poor reflection as in a mirror; then we shall see face to face. Now I know in part; then I shall know fully, even as I am fully known. I will have the answers to every one of my questions. It won't be as if the questions didn't matter or that I wasn't worthy of the answers.

God also redeemed me through time. The season of grief is still with me but it is not as burdensome. I can laugh and enjoy life with my family without the profound sense of sadness. I still talk with Craig and God. Sometimes these conversations are out on the driveway as the sun sets. Sometimes they are at other times of the day.

With one exception, I have not had another conversation with those people who left messages for me in that first week. Our friends are almost entirely among those who have had similar losses as ours. Time continues to work miracles as my healing continues.

I still miss my Craig. I am still angry that I can't hold him, touch him, or hear about the latest happening in his life. I ache that we are not together, but I know that we will be some day.

Week Two
"WHY?"

WEEK TWO
"WHY?"

Harold Ivan Smith has said,

> "Why
> Is more of a paragraph than a word;
> Is more of a lament than a question."[3]

We long to know the reason our child died or who is to blame for our child's death. Maybe, if we knew there was just reason, we could better accept it.

In our hearts and minds, could there ever be reason enough? Just cause doesn't exist. Our children didn't deserve to die. We don't deserve the suffering.

Our hearts beg for an answer where there isn't one. We are so programmed for, "If you're good, you'll be blessed. If you're bad, you'll be cursed." It's learned at a very early age. Santa Claus is making a list! It's even taught in church. God punishes the sinful and rewards the righteous. There are scriptures that, if taken out of context, suggest to us that the faithful get all they pray for. What parent doesn't pray for their children and their safety from accident and illness?

Most of us know enough of the Bible to quote a few verses. We know the basic stories and the main characters. We can recite a few of our favorite promises. We use some verses like clichés. We put them on plaques on our walls and find them a great source of encouragement. Then our child dies.

We've heard many grieving parents say, "God will never give you more than you can handle." Yet, their hearts scream, "This is way more than I can handle!" So, God either doesn't really know us or He's just plain mean and likes to see us squirm. We will examine this cliché later.

All we want is what's fair. Job questioned God's fairness. He asked God to explain Himself (Job 13). He questioned God, "How many wrongs and sins have I committed? Show me my offense and sin." **Why??** To question why is a lament of the soul. It's not fair. It's grossly unfair for our children to die before we do.

[3]*Alive Now Magazine*, Sept./Oct. 1982 pg. 7

DAY 1: IT WAS GOD'S PLAN

Open each day's study with this prayer or one of your own:

"Almighty God of our salvation, your love and grace are steadfast.
Come near to us in our turmoil; carry us with your Holy Word.
Allow us to enter into your gates with the assurance
that we can set our lives against despair and death."

Amen

"Why?" is the most heart wrenching question asked by those of us who are at the depths of despair. We need a reason. When the answers aren't so clear-cut, we strive for one we can at least accept. If you can accept that it was God's plan, so be it. That's probably the most common reason expressed by the believer. We aren't trying to change your mind or persuade you in any way. However, we'd like to introduce and work through the scripture most often used to support this opinion. We'd like for you to know what you believe *and* to be able to support it from the Bible.

Read Psalm 139: 1-18

Verses 1-6 (NIV) Please fill in the blanks:

"O LORD, you have searched me and you _____ me. You _____ when I sit and when I rise; you _____ my thoughts from afar. You _____ my going out and my lying down; you are_____ with all of my ways. Before a word is on my tongue you _____ it completely, O LORD. You hem me in—behind and before; you have laid your hand upon me. Such _____is too wonderful for me, too lofty for me to attain.

Verses 13-16 (NIV)

"For you created me in my inmost being;
you knit me together in my
mother's womb.
I praise you because I am fearfully
and wonderfully made;
your works are wonderful,
I know that full well.
My frame was not hidden from you

> when I was made in the secret place.
> When I was woven together in the
> depths of the earth,
> your eyes saw my unformed body.
> All the days ordained for me
> were written in your book
> before one of them came to be."

Psalm 139: 16 (Amplified)

"Your eyes saw my unformed substance and in your book all the days [of my life] were written before ever they took shape, when as yet there was none of them."

From verse 16, some people draw the conclusion that God has a plan for our life—that God plans the number of our days. You've heard some people say, "It was their time to go." This Psalm does not use the word plan. It does clearly state that God *knows* the number of our days. The NIV's use of the phrase "All the days ordained for me", suggests that the span of life is sovereignly determined and recorded in the heavenly royal register of God's decisions.[4]

Psalm 139: 16 (KJV)

> "Thine eyes did see my substance, yet being unperfect;
> And in thy book all members were written,
> Which in continuance were fashioned,
> When as yet there was none of them."

1. How does this change the meaning for you of verse 16, or does it?

Strong's Concordance for verse 16 defines members as from the Hebrew word yatsur which means limb or part of a structure that was molded or fashioned; especially as a potter.2

When you read verse 16 within the context of the entire Psalm, we understand that the psalmist was praising God for the complexity of his own existence. George Knight in his commentary on this Psalm for verses 1-6 states as speaking for the psalmist, "For my part, I don't know what I am going to say before I open my mouth. You know every

---

[4]NIV text note page 944; NIV Study Bible, Copyright 1985, 1995, 2002 by the Zondervan Corporation

detail about the flow of my sentences, their superficial sound, their real meaning, their connection with my attitude to life, my faith, or even lack of it. There you are Lord, in front of me and behind me in space, as well as before me in time, and after me also, after I experience this moment and then can look back upon it. I cannot put back the clock to escape you, or put it forward to an unthinkable future. But apart from "before" and "after", at this very moment your hand lies on my head in blessing (verse 5). I have discovered that I am fenced in by you, fenced in by your love. Verse 6 then gives us an exclamation, not of fear and horror, but of reverent awe at the mystery of such a wonderful God."3

God knows everything about us. He knows all the intricacies and what we are made of, even to our unique DNA. He's known about us for centuries and knows the days we have left to live. He knows how our life fits in the grand scheme of the master plan. He records everything about us including every tear we shed (Psalm 56:8).

Having said that, he doesn't give us the words to say. We aren't puppets on a string. Our thoughts are our own and we are responsible for how we live our lives and the choices we make. We have free will to choose to live in harmony with the rest of God's creation and to accept His love for us or not accept this gift.

Read Jeremiah 29: 11-13

Verse 29: 11 (NIV) Please fill in the blanks:

"For I know the _____ I have for you," declares the Lord, "_____ to prosper you and not harm you_____ to give you hope and a future."

2. Do you believe the death of your child was God's plan? If so, what scriptures support your belief? What you believe is between you and God. All we ask is that you have prayed about it and are able to support it in scripture through Bible study—not for argument's sake but for your sake. Remember that everyone does not have to agree if you are within a small group. Listen to each other, but allow God to inform your personal journey. You may not know what you believe at this point and what you believe may change over the course of this study. Be patient.

5James Strong, Abingdon's Strong's Exhaustive Concordance of the Bible, ©1986 by Abingdon Press, pg. 67 of the Hebrew and Chaldee Dictionary of the Old Testament (3338 & 3335).
6George A. F. Knight, The Daily Study Bible Series/Psalms Volume 2, © G. A. F. Knight 1983, published by The Saint Andrew Press, Edinburgh, Scotland and Westminster John Knox Press, Louisville , Kentucky, pg.320

DAY 2: PUNISHMENT FOR SINS OR LACK OF RIGHT LIVING

Opening Prayer:

"Almighty God of our salvation, your love and grace are steadfast.
Come near to us in our turmoil; carry us with your Holy Word.
Allow us to enter into your gates with the assurance
that we can set our lives against despair and death."

Amen

Job's friends were insistent that Job's suffering was due to some sin for which Job had not repented.

Read Job 8: 1-7

1. What did Bildad accuse Job's children of doing?

Bildad tells Job that his children must have sinned, and if Job would repent of those sins, God would restore him to his rightful place.

Read Job 22: 5-11

2. What does Eliphaz say is the cause of Job's suffering?

Eliphaz reprimands Job for his gross social sins against the needy, those who are naked and hungry, the widows and the fatherless. The only proof Eliphaz has for Job's alleged wickedness is his present suffering. It's not true.

Read Job 11: 13-20

3. From what does Zophar believe Job's problems stem?

Zophar assumes that Job's problems are rooted in his sin, and all that Job has to do is repent and he will be restored.

Read Job 1:8 (NIV) Please fill in the blanks:

"Then the Lord said to Satan, 'Have you considered my servant Job? There is no one on earth like him; he is

_____ and_____, a man who _____ _____and

_____ _____.'"

4. What does God say about Job?

God says that Job is blameless and righteous. Job's suffering is not due to his sin or his children's sins. We'll visit Job again, but for now, we need to understand that sin was not the reason for Job's suffering.

Read John 9: 1-3

5. What question did the disciples ask Jesus?

They wanted to know who sinned to cause the man's blindness.

What was Jesus' reply? (verse 3)

Jesus plainly contradicts the belief that sin caused the man's blindness. Neither the man nor his parents sinned.

6. Do you believe that your child died because God is punishing you or your child for some sin committed? If so, what scripture supports your belief?

DAY 3: LACK OF FAITH

Opening prayer:

"Almighty God of our salvation, your love and grace are steadfast.
Come near to us in our turmoil; carry us with your Holy Word.
Allow us to enter into your gates with the assurance
that we can set our lives against despair and death."

Amen

Elaine actually had someone in her Sunday school class say to her, "If my child died, I would have to believe that it was because my faith wasn't strong enough to save him."

Read Hebrews 11: 1

1. What is faith?

Faith is being sure of what we hope for and certain of what we do not see. It is believing in God.

Read Matthew 7: 7

 Matthew 21: 21, 22

 John 15: 7

 John 14: 3

It appears we can hand God our wish list, and it will be given to us. We prayed daily for all three of our children and believed that God would protect each of them. So what happened? What happened is that Craig is protected—just not in the way we had expected when we prayed.

Many believe that when people become believers, nothing bad will ever happen to them again. And yet, when Jesus was in the Garden of Gethsemane, he prayed in faith that he would not have to go through with the suffering of the cross. Jesus' faith didn't falter. Jesus' suffering was not because he lacked faith.

Read Acts 6: 8

2. What kind of man was Stephen?

He was a man full of God's grace and power. He did great wonders and miraculous signs among the people. He was a believer with great faith.

Read Acts 7: 54-8: 1

3. What happened to Stephen?

He was stoned to death because of his faith.

Read Acts 12: 1-2

4. What happened to the disciples? What happened to the disciple James, the brother of John?

They were persecuted for their faith and James was put to death. They were men of great faith and yet they were not free from trouble.

Read John 16: 33

5. Does Jesus promise a trouble-free faith?

Jesus says the complete opposite. In this world, we will have trouble. He also assures us, "But take heart! I have overcome the world."

6. Do you believe that the death of your child was because you lacked faith? If so, what scripture supports your belief?

DAY 4: GOD IS POWERLESS TO PREVENT DEATH

Opening Prayer:

"Almighty God of our salvation, your love and grace are steadfast.
Come near to us in our turmoil; carry us with your Holy Word.
Allow us to enter into your gates with the assurance
that we can set our lives against despair and death."

Amen

We personally don't believe that God caused Craig's death. However, He allowed it to happen. He could have delayed their car at a stoplight for five seconds. He could have prevented the other car's driver from ignoring a stop sign. God could have made it rain that day so that the boys couldn't work and would have stayed home. There are so many ways that God could have intervened that fateful day but didn't. And yet, who's to say that God didn't intervene a million times or more in Craig's eighteen years of life. The question is: what happened this time?

In our years of ministry, we've heard it said many times, "God was surely with him/her," when someone narrowly escapes death. Why wasn't God "with" Craig? We believe He was.

Read Matthew 26: 52-54

Verse 26: 53 (NIV) Please fill in the blanks:

"Do you think I cannot call on my Father, and _____ _____ _____ _____

_____ _____ _____ _____ more than twelve legions of angels."

Jesus knew he could call on God's power. He also knew there was a purpose in fulfilling the scriptures. Jesus trusted in that purpose through his faithful obedience.

We get into trouble when we try to use only human reasoning to understand the purposes of God.

Read Isaiah 55: 6-11

Verse 55: 8 (NIV) Please fill in the blanks:

"For _____ _____ are not _____ _____neither are

_____ _____ _____ _____declares the Lord."

Verse 55: 11 (NIV) Please fill in the blanks:

"so is my word that goes out from my mouth; it will _____ _____ _____

_____ _____ but will _____ what I _____ and achieve the

_____ for which _____ _____ _____."

Jesus' life, death, and resurrection fulfill a purpose God alone could see. Jesus' death accomplished a greater good not only for us but for Jesus himself.

1. Do you believe God was powerless to prevent your child's death? If so, what scripture supports your belief?

DAY 5: GOD IS NOT LOVING

Opening Prayer:

"Almighty God of our salvation, your love and grace are steadfast.
Come near to us in our turmoil; carry us with your Holy Word.
Allow us to enter into your gates with the assurance
that we can set our lives against despair and death."
                                                        Amen

If God doesn't love, He must be cruel and heartless. Obviously, that is not true. However, sometimes we feel abandoned by God. We feel he has turned his back on us and that he doesn't care. We don't feel loved by God. We feel if God really loved us, he wouldn't allow the depth of suffering that the death of our child causes. A loving Father simply doesn't do that.

It's possible it wasn't about us. It's possible it was for Craig's greater good. We won't know God's thoughts until we reach heaven ourselves. We can only trust in the wisdom of God and know his ways are above our ways.

Read 1 Corinthians 13: 12-13

This we can know fully—God loves our child and each of us. Craig is safe in that "better place". There was purpose in his death that is impossible for us to know, but we can trust in a loving God.

Read Luke 22: 39-46

Verse 22: 42 (NIV) Please fill in the blanks:

"Father, if you are willing, take this cup from me; yet not _____ will, _____ _____ be done."

Why did Jesus relent to his Father's will?

Jesus didn't relent to his father's will because he felt his father was mean and heartless. He relented because of his deep-seated trust in his father's love and wisdom.

Verse 22: 43 (NIV) Please fill in the blanks:

"An _____ from heaven appeared to him and _____ him.

1. Who sent the angel and why?

God sent the angel to strengthen Jesus. God could have simply removed the trial, but he didn't. Only God can see the bigger picture or the grand scheme. Jesus trusted that God's wisdom would prevail over his trial.

2. In verses 40 and 46, what did Jesus tell his disciples to pray for?

He told them to pray that they will not fall into temptation. They didn't understand. They kept falling asleep.

Verse 22: 44 (NIV) Please fill in the blanks:

"And being in _____, he prayed more earnestly, and _____ _____

_____ _____ _____ _____

_____ falling to the ground."

There is a condition called hematidrosis which is the actual mingling of blood and sweat which can occur in times of extreme anguish, strain, or sensitivity. Only Luke the doctor records this happening to Jesus.[7]

---

[7]NIV text note, Zondervan NIV Study Bible, © 1985, 1995, 2002 by Zondervan Corporation, pg. 1616

Jesus was in extreme anguish and yet he was able to relinquish himself to his father's will. He could not have done this had he not trusted in his father's love, wisdom, and purpose. Jesus agreed to come to us knowing full well what he would have to do.

Read John 3: 16

This is probably the first scripture we learned as children. It is foundational to the Christian faith. Sometimes it is so familiar that we take it for granted.

Read 1 John 4: 7-17

1 John 4: 16 (NIV) Please fill in the blanks:

"And so we know and rely on the love God has for us. _____ _____

_____. Whoever lives in _____ lives in _____, and

_____ in _____."

God is love. We understand this best in the unconditional love we have for our own children. God is the love we have in our hearts for them.

Read Ephesians 3: 14-19

3. Do you trust in God's love for you?

Life's Not Fair — by Elaine

My 15-year-old nephew, Steven, died in a freak accident 15 years ago from which he should have maybe suffered a broken arm, and yet he died. He fell 4 feet off the back of a barely moving car. He hit his head on the curb of the street and crushed his brain stem. Kids fall all the time. People have survived falls of 40-50 feet from the ground. How is it possible for a kid to fall 4 feet and die?

My brother, Ron, died from a stroke at the age of 47 on December 24, 1999, just 6 months before Craig died. How does a strong, physically fit man of 47 die from a stroke? Old people have a stroke and often recover. My brothers, sisters, and I traveled to Phoenix, Arizona for the funeral leaving our families in Missouri to celebrate Christmas without us. I missed celebrating Craig's last Christmas with him.

I was afraid. We are a Christian family—all of us. There are 8 children in my family and 3 of us have lost children as well as a brother.

Three months after my brother's death my niece died. She was almost 15. However, she only had brain- stem function from the age of 3 months. She never talked, walked, or played with a toy. She was cruelly labeled a vegetable for all but 3 months of her life. I have a lot of "WHYs".

Life holds no guarantees. Life isn't fair. Life stinks. All the clichés have an element of truth in each of them. That simply isn't reason enough for this kind of reality.

I arrived home from Ron's funeral on December 29th. On New Year's Eve, Craig asked if he could go "out and about" with friends. The town we lived in was very small. We gave him permission with conditions. He had to be home by 1:00 a.m. and stay in town. Even though Craig was 17, he had a curfew. All our boys had a curfew until they graduated from high school. I couldn't sleep until they were home safe. They argued sometimes but always complied. If they were going to be late, they knew to call me.

So, when Craig wasn't home by 1:00, I started to worry. When it was 1:15, I sent his brother out to look for him. Our town was so small that he could have walked home by then. By 1:30, I started calling other parents. When a couple of his closest friends weren't home either, I knew who he was with but I didn't know where. We hadn't had trouble with Craig before but I was starting to panic. My brother had just died. My mind was going everywhere it shouldn't go. Maybe he was lying in a ditch hurt because he had left town. Maybe he was drinking. We hadn't caught him drinking before, but he was 17, and it was New Year's Eve. His brother couldn't find him. Where could he be? I had David call the police to see if there were any reported accidents. It was so unlike Craig to miss curfew. He knew how upset I was following my brother's death. He was a good kid. Why hadn't he at least called? Something terrible must have happened!

Finally, about 1:45, he came home. "Where have you been!?" I asked. I didn't know whether to hug him or hit him. He said, "I'm sorry Mom. Joe, Brad, Chris, and I were out driving around. We got to talking about God and stuff." I asked, "Why didn't you call me?" Craig said, "It was a serious conversation and I thought it would spoil the moment." Of all the things that I thought might have happened, witnessing with friends about his faith never crossed my mind. Shame on me!

I asked him what they talked about. He said they were talking about how there could be a God when so many bad things happen. I asked Craig what he said. He told me that he had told them, "If nothing bad ever happens to you, you don't need any faith." Wow! Six months before Craig died, he told me what faith **really** means.

Recently, I came across this quotation from a weblog by Bill Tammeus. It was actually written by a friend of his, Paul Jones. Paul is Trappist monk and lives as a hermit in rural Missouri. Paul wrote an article for the magazine Weavings and the following is a small portion of the article:

> "Faith is unavoidable, for to live entails wagering on some 'vision.' No matter how shallow or deep, how narrow or expansive, whether chosen or imposed, something that renders it better to live than to die must engage our trust. The 'proof' of our vision is the quality of life that results from risking our life and death on it. Faith resides in the deep human need for a unifying passion in the face of all objective uncertainty. It follows that the heart of Christian living is the single-mindedness of an undivided heart, a heart so completely gambling on its vision that nothing makes sense if God does not exist. Faithfulness means living this vision 'as if' it were so, in order to make it so."

"Faith doesn't mean having all the answers. Faith is to live confidently without all the answers, trusting our destiny and the destiny of all creation to the hands of a God whose very heart is love," writes Tammeus on his blog.

Call it a journey or pilgrimage, but the road back to a healthy faith has been a long one for me. It was well worth it. I say with a confident heart that God is love. I know God loves Craig and me. I know it.

•••

Why? — by David

In the first couple of weeks after Craig's accident, I remember being given two separate pieces of advice. One was don't try to figure out who's in charge and the second piece of advice was to spend as little time as possible with the "Why?" questions. "There are simply no answers", I was told. I have tried to follow the latter advice even if, at times, I have wondered if there is in fact an order to this world of ours. It is a dilemma that bereaved parents know all too well. In fact, the same bereaved father made both comments to me.

I did pretty well in avoiding the why questions but they did creep inside my head. The world didn't seem as friendly, predictable, or dependable as it had before Craig's accident. I still cringe when our kids leave our home after a visit. The sight of crosses along the roadside breaks my heart.

I had thought that my faith was reasonably solid. After all, I am a pastor. I recall silently scoffing at a person who talked to me one day about some hardships in his life. He expressed to me that he thought being a Christian was supposed to shield him from such troubles. I thought to myself, "Where did you get such an idea?" But I realized in those early months of grief that I had acted as if that was the truth.

I repeatedly asked God, "Why me? Why us? Had I not done your will? Haven't I been faithful to your leading?" I became ashamed the first time I realized that I had fallen into a self-serving view of God and Creation. I said that I didn't believe being a disciple would protect me from life's difficult times, but I certainly responded as if I felt that way.

There is a lot that I haven't figured out yet, but this much is clear—the grief following the death of a loved one is intensified by a great amount of bad theology. The death of a loved one also creates an enormous amount of bad theology. Our lives, for the most part, are not tested or challenged. We accept ideas as being true and don't really wrestle with them until we are forced to do so. We misquote scripture. We rip Bible verses out of their context and get only partial understanding. All of which leads us to a place where we believe that God is distant and uncaring.

In that first year after Craig's death, I tried hard not to engage in the "Why?" speculation, but I was only partially successful. A turning point for me came the morning of Good Friday, 2001.

I woke from a night of sleep to a mind that was already racing. "It's Good Friday," I thought to myself while still in bed. Immediately I heard a voice inside my head say, "Don't call the day my Son died good."

I let that thought sink in for awhile and then began to wonder if I would ever get any answers to my questions. My first thought was that I probably wouldn't. The answers wouldn't come in this lifetime. They are much too deep. The answers to the "Why?" questions are too much mystery.

Ok, I thought to myself. Maybe I'll understand when I get to heaven. No, I answered myself. Then I will be with Craig, Dad, and all the others and why won't matter. For a brief moment, I resigned myself that these questions must be something I simply wasn't meant to understand, but then God spoke to me again.

I thought of I Corinthians 13: 12. To this day, I know that this verse was brought into my remembrance by God. It is not a verse that I would by myself have considered. The verse says, "Now we see but a poor reflection as in a mirror; then we shall see face to face. Now I know in part; then I shall know fully, even as I am fully known." I may not have all things related to Craig's death figured out but there will come a time in eternity when I will know fully. I will know the answers to my why questions. There will come a time when God will honor my requests because he loves me.

Not everyone I have shared this story with agrees with my interpretation of the verse in Corinthians. That's all right with me. I know this is from God because it has provided peace and direction in my journey. Some of the whys have become clearer to me during the intervening time. I know that God's love will hold me accountable and will provide the understanding that I so long for in this lifetime.

Not all the whys are answered, but my soul is much calmer.

Week Three

WHAT HAPPENS WHEN WE DIE? — GLIMPSES OF HEAVEN

WEEK THREE
WHAT HAPPENS WHEN WE DIE? — GLIMPSES OF HEAVEN
by Elaine

I used to go out on my back patio at night and gaze up at the moon and stars. I would wonder where Craig was. What was he doing? Where was the "better place" called heaven, and what did it look like? Does he look the same? Will I recognize him when I get there? What will our relationship look like? Will I still be his mom?

Was Craig somewhere beyond the stars, or was he right there beside me, close enough to reach out and touch, but not feel or see? I would think that if I could simply see him from afar, as if looking through a window, that I could be at peace with him being gone. I needed to know that he was OK. Was he so happy that he wouldn't want to come back?

Of course, I can't have that "window" of opportunity. However, God has assured me that Craig is safe with Him. The glimpses of heaven that are offered in scripture have become a great comfort to me. I believe Craig is in paradise with God. I believe it is better than I could ever hope for or imagine. It's more than I could provide. God is love. In Him there is no darkness. Craig is more than OK.

Craig was created for a relationship with God. We tried to raise Craig with a desire to spend eternity with Him. It's hard to imagine and accept that there is a love greater than mine. There is. I still miss him terribly and long for a hug. Only God can give him paradise.

DAY 1: MANY MANSIONS

Open each day's study with this prayer or one of your own:

"Living God, our lives have lost their contours and we are lost.
We are cut to the quick and yet feel nothing.
Our world seems familiar and alien at the same time.
Give us your light to guide our footsteps, and direct us to your truth."

Amen

The scriptures tell us about a place that is filled with God's presence. This place is where the perfect Reign of God exists. It is filled with divinely created beings. It is called heaven. While the scripture gives us a few concrete details about this place, it is, for the most part, vague about many of the details. We are going to take a brief survey of what we know to be true about our heavenly home and what it might be like.

Read John 14

Verse 14: 1 (NIV) Please fill in the blanks:

Do not let your _____ be _____. Trust in _____; trust also in

_____.

John 14 is the record of a teaching moment that Jesus had with his disciples shortly before his arrest and crucifixion. Jesus has just told his disciples that he would not be with them much longer and that before the next dawn Peter would deny being a disciple of the Christ.

Since the disciples had just received words that disturbed them greatly, Jesus begins this part of his conversation with words intended to comfort. "Don't let your hearts be troubled," he said. He then goes on to give his prescription for a troubled heart: "trust in God, trust also in me".

John 14: 2 (NIV) Please fill in the blank:

In my Father's house are many _____; if it were not so, I would have told you. I am going there to

prepare a place for you.

John 14: 3 (NIV) Please fill in the blanks:

And if I go and prepare a place for you, I will come back and _____ _____ _____

_____ _____ _____ that you also may be _____ _____ _____.

1. Who is talking? What is the setting?

Jesus is comforting and reassuring his disciples in the large upper room provided for them in order to share the last supper (Mark 14: 12-15) hours before Jesus' crucifixion.

2. What is the glimpse of heaven we see from John 14: 2?

From this passage we perceive that heaven is a physical place with "rooms" prepared by Jesus for those he calls his disciples. We are provided a glimpse of heaven as a physical place where God is as well as where Jesus is going. In this passage, the disciples closest to Jesus don't know what is about to take place but Jesus, in his compassion, gives his disciples the assurance that they will be together again.

3. How does this passage reflect heaven for you?

DAY 2: THE SEA IS NO MORE

Opening Prayer:

"Living God, our lives have lost their contours and we are lost.
We are cut to the quick and yet feel nothing.
Our world seems familiar and alien at the same time.
Give us your light to guide our footsteps, and direct us to your truth."

Amen

Read Revelation 21: 1-8

New Jerusalem, the home of God and those who have survived the trials and tribulations of the world, is described in word pictures that stir the soul. It is the home created by God for his people. In this new creation, certain things will not exist. Things such as death, mourning, crying or pain will not be a part of heaven. It is the deepest expression of the intimate fellowship that God had promised to those in covenant relationship with him.

Verse 21: 1 (NIV) Please fill in the blanks:

"Then I saw a new _____ and a new earth for the first _____ and the first

_____ had passed away, and there was no longer any _____."

What do you think "the sea" represents in this passage?

The phrase "the sea" is a technical term that represents chaos, or separation from God. It also represents a force or enemy hostile to God.[8] Without divine intervention, the sea overwhelms humans with its savage power. In the Gospels, Jesus controls the stormy sea with just his words. John of the Revelation points out that the unruly, chaotic parts of our lives will not exist in the New Jerusalem. He points out that all things will be under the power and rule of God.

[8]*The Daily Bible Series, the Revelation of John volume 2* by William Barclay, published by Westminster Press, © 1976 William Barclay, pgs. 197-199.

1. Name those parts of your life that are out of control or chaotic or those parts that you might describe as a "storm of life".

Verse 21: 3b (NIV) Please fill in the blanks:

"Now the dwelling of God is _____ _____, and he will _____ with them. They will be _____ _____, and God himself will be _____ _____ and be their God.

2. What glimpse of heaven does this passage give us?

Again, heaven seems to be a place (New Jerusalem). Yesterday we looked at a verse from John's gospel that spoke of the eternal relationship God desires with his people. John continues this thought in this verse where he says that in the new creation of God, God himself will be with men (humankind) and God will live with them. They will be his people and God himself will be with them to be their God.

3. Does this glimpse of heaven bring you comfort?

DAY 3: "TODAY YOU WILL BE WITH ME IN PARADISE"

Opening Prayer:

"Living God, our lives have lost their contours and we are lost.
We are cut to the quick and yet feel nothing.
Our world seems familiar and alien at the same time.
Give us your light to guide our footsteps, and direct us to your truth."

Amen

Read Luke 23: 39-43

We often talk as if heaven is a place, but some consider it to be a blessed state of existence or a blissful state of being. In our Old Testament the word translated "paradise" means garden or forest. According to The Strongest Concordance[9] the word used for "paradise" here and at 2 Corinthians 12:4, and Revelation 2:7 means "a place of blessedness, from the base meaning of garden".

1. Are these words of Jesus meant to be taken literally? Are we taken immediately into God's presence after our death?

2. What do the words, "today you will be with me in paradise," mean to you?

---

[9]*The Strongest NIV Exhaustive Concordance* by Edward W. Goodrick and John R. Kohlenberger III, © 1999, 1990 by Zondervan, pg. 1579

3. What is "paradise" to you? Is it a physical place, a relationship with God, a state of rest till the second coming, or something else to you?

4. Does your belief in heaven or paradise give you comfort?

According to Barclay's commentary this verse's importance is that Jesus promised the thief on the cross next to him an honored place of a companion in the garden of the courts of heaven. He also says that surely this story tells us above all that it is never too late to turn to Christ.[10]

[10]*The Daily Bible Series, the Gospel of Luke* by William Barclay, published by Westminster Press, © 1975 William Barclay, pg. 287

DAY 4: SEARCHING FOR THE LIVING AMONG THE DEAD

Opening Prayer:

"Living God, our lives have lost their contours and we are lost.
We are cut to the quick and yet feel nothing.
Our world seems familiar and alien at the same time.
Give us your light to guide our footsteps, and direct us to your truth."

Amen

Read Luke 24: 1-8

Verse 24: 5 (NIV) Please fill in the blanks:

"In their fright the women bowed down with their faces to the ground, but the men said to them, "Why do you look

for the _____ among the _____.

The men in clothes that gleamed like lightning asked the women why they were searching for the living among the

dead.

1. Where were the women and who were the men speaking about?

They were at the tomb and, of course, the men were speaking about Jesus. The women had witnessed the whole

thing. They saw Jesus die a horrendous death on the cross. They fully expected to find Jesus in the tomb. Who

would think he would be anywhere else? They were frightened when they found the men in clothes that gleamed like

lightening. Then they were asked a question that had to confuse them even more.

2. What did the question mean?

It really wasn't a question. It was a statement that Jesus had been resurrected and is now alive!

Verse 24: 6 (NIV) Please fill in the blanks:

"He is _____ _____; he has _____!"

Remember how he told you, while he was still with you in Galilee: 7 "The Son of Man must be delivered into the hands of sinful men, be crucified and on the third day be raised again." Then they remembered his words.

3. Jesus is described as "living". What does that mean to you? What promise are we given for those who believe?

We, too, are promised a life of living in a place called heaven.

Read Luke 24: 50-53

Verse 24: 51 (NIV) Please fill in the blanks:

While he was blessing them, he left them and was _____ _____ _____ _____.

4. Where does this verse suggest heaven is?

Jesus went up in the sky, somewhere above. It also suggests heaven is with the Father and in "glory".

Verse 24:52 (NIV) Please fill in the blanks:

Then they _____ him and returned to Jerusalem with great _____.

Finally they understood and were blessed with peace and great joy even though Jesus was leaving them.

DAY 5: HE WHO OVERCOMES—THE TREE OF LIFE

Opening Prayer:

"Living God, our lives have lost their contours and we are lost.
We are cut to the quick and yet feel nothing.
Our world seems familiar and alien at the same time.
Give us your light to guide our footsteps, and direct us to your truth."

Amen

Read Genesis 1: 31-2: 3

God had finished his creation and saw all that He had made and it was very good. God rested on the seventh day, not because he was tired, but because nothing empty or formless remained. His creative work was complete—and it was totally effective and absolutely perfect. He called it "very good"

Read Genesis 2:8-25

Genesis 2:8 (NIV) Please fill in the blanks:

Now the Lord God had planted a garden in the east, in Eden' and there _____ _____

_____ _____ he had formed.

1. What was God's desire for human existence?

God's will and desire for all of us is to live with him in perfection, in a perfect place of great beauty, and paradise.

Read Revelation 1: 9-11

We read in Revelation 1:1 that this book is the revelation of Jesus Christ, which God gave him to show his servants what must soon take place. These are believed to be the words of Jesus given to John to record. Verse 11 instructs John to write the words on a scroll and send it to the seven churches. There is a formula he uses for each church. He tells them that he has certain things "for" them and certain things "against" them. Then Jesus tells each church to repent and what they must do or suffer some consequences. Finally, he tells each church, "He who has an ear, let him hear, what the Spirit says to the churches. To him who overcomes…"

Read Revelation 2: 7 (NIV)   Please fill in the blanks:

To _____ who overcomes, I will give the right to _____ from the _____

_____ _____, which is in the _____ of God.

2. What does God give to those who overcome and are victorious in the battle against sin?

He gives him (us) life in paradise. Here the word paradise is originally a Persian word for a pleasure garden. In Revelation it symbolizes the eschatological state in which God and believers are restored to the perfect fellowship that existed before sin entered the world.

3. What is the significance of the seven churches?

The seven churches are located about 50 miles apart, forming a circle in Asia moving clockwise north from Ephesus to Laodicea. Seven is a number of completeness or fullness.

4. What is the significance of the use of the singular "to him" who overcomes?

Even though the words are given to the churches, each individual must battle sin. Put yourself in each of the church settings, and ask yourself if God could have certain things for or against you, then repent and receive the blessing of overcoming.

5. What does it mean to you to have the right to eat from the Tree of Life?

Craig in Glory —by Elaine

The time between Craig's death and funeral is a blur. I remember bits and pieces of those five days. I remember the anguish of not knowing where Craig might be. Was he safe? Was he gone for good or was he in the "better place" called heaven? Would I really see him again? Was he a ghost floating around my room and I simply couldn't see him? I couldn't rest. I *needed* to know.

My prayers were desperate. I had to know he was OK. As many of you know, rational thought is almost nonexistent in those first few weeks. At least that is what it was like for me. I wanted to run but I didn't have a place to go. I literally had to force myself to stay in the house. I had to find him. Maybe, I simply wanted to run from the reality I couldn't face. My mind raced on and on. I had to have answers. I had **huge** faith issues.

It was torment. However, there were also moments of God's grace. I can't remember where or when, but God gave me a "glimpse" of Craig in glory. I had a vision of Craig without clothes except a white cloth across the front of him. He had a glow surrounding him especially his head. He wasn't in a place. It was as if he was on his way somewhere else. I've tried to discount the vision as wishful thinking.

I have since come to the realization that it really was a vision from God. Craig was 18 when he died. I hadn't seen him naked for many years. If I had "pictured" Craig, I would have pictured him with clothes on. I would have pictured a place. I have also come to realize that I received peace from the vision. It had to be God. It was not what I would have imagined. It was and is peace without understanding.

There is a wonderful verse in 1 Corinthians 2: 9

However, as it is written:

"No eye has seen,
no ear has heard,
no mind has conceived
what God has prepared for those who love him."

I am no longer troubled by where Craig is. I don't know the details, but I know that he is safe and in a paradise that I can't even imagine. God is a god of comfort, and I trust in his love for me and for Craig. Craig is in a good place prepared by Jesus himself. I am grateful.

•••

Talking and Listening — by David

A few months ago, I was visiting with the owner of a local Christian bookstore. While we were talking, a man who I had just met for the first time, about three days earlier, came into the store. When we had met for that first time, this man asked me if I had read Heaven by Randy Alcorn. I said I had not. "Oh, it's so good," he said. "I'll loan you my copy the next time we get together." When he saw me at the store, he actually purchased the book for me.

Now, the truth is I have started the book, but I haven't gotten very far into it. I plan to finish the book, but it, along with several others, are partially read and are waiting their turn on my bookshelf. My lack of progress is not because I am not interested in the subject. It's the lack of time that keeps me from finishing them.

Craig's accident is the measuring rod for what I believe. It has thrust me beyond an easy belief system. So, I wonder what do I really know and believe about the afterlife.

Since Craig's death, I have held onto the belief that he is in Heaven. I know that he was a believing Christian. For me, that means he is "saved by grace through faith in Jesus Christ." I always admired his conviction and his willingness to live the faith, as well as, verbally share his faith.

The accident thrust both Elaine and me on a spiritual journey. Both of us have learned to think seriously and critically about all facets of our faith. What does it mean to pray? Is God truly loving? Do miracles really happen? Are miracles real for today's world? Little by little over the last decade, we have framed our questions and learned to lean on God's grace for direction.

So, what do I believe about eternity? I believe that we live in a relational world. Jesus tells us that just as this world is filled with relationships, eternity will also be filled with relationships. I understand that God calls each of his children by name to eternity.

> Eternity is a place where God himself wipes away our tears.
> God himself gives our grief validity.

I know that I have had the honor of being with dear saints of God as the moment of death drew near. I remember listening to one side of a conversation between a parishioner and his deceased son. This man had been on his deathbed for a few days. On this particular day, after several hours of unresponsiveness, he opened his eyes and with a look of peace began to talk to someone. There was obviously a conversation going with someone else. His voice was clear and resonant as he talked. His eyes were fixed on the ceiling. Eventually he mentioned a name, and all of us in the room turned to his adult daughter. She was obviously touched by all of this. The daughter looked at us and whispered, "He's talking to my brother." Now, I knew from earlier conversations with this man, that he held much guilt and grief concerning his ten-year-old son who died of burns from a house fire. A holy pall cast itself over all of us. This man, after fifty plus years of mourning, was having a conversation with his son. Truly a holy mystery.

A few years ago, I was pacing up and down my driveway talking to God and Craig. Elaine and I had moved to a new parish, and I had just told Craig that our new setting of ministry was actually a very beautiful place. Immediately, I heard Craig say, "It's more beautiful here." All I could do was smile and sigh.

I want my belief about eternity, resurrection, heaven, hell, and all things pertaining to life eternal to be scripturally informed. I yearn to understand better what God's promises mean, and I take a quiet confidence in the faith that I currently have regarding the afterlife.

I look forward to learning more here on earth about the living Spirit of my son.

❧

Week Four

WORDS OF OTHERS

WEEK FOUR
WORDS OF OTHERS

The words of other people can at times keep us from understanding the truth. We let the expectations of others dictate how we grieve. When those others are trusted friends or respected authorities - such as a pastor - we tend to allow them to think for us.

Early in our grief, we truly are in a weakened state. It's difficult to think or reason, much less think straight. The words of others can be extremely helpful and comforting. When they are not, we can remember that most people mean well and are only trying to help.

However, there comes a time when we need to search the Bible on our own and seek the heart of the Comforter. He will lead us to the truth and understanding. Rely on Him. He may work through others but don't let them put words in His mouth. His words are supported in scripture. He is the Word (John 1).

Often conversations begin something like this, "The Bible says…". The person will speak with great conviction but when you ask for the specific reference, they are unable to provide it to you. This doesn't necessarily make them wrong, but it should encourage you to check it out for yourself. The goal of this study is for you to know what you believe and be able to support it in scripture. Don't take our word for it or anyone else's as your only source of information.

As mentioned before, this study guide is meant as just that—a guide. We believe that all scripture is God breathed. Said another way, we believe that the Bible is God-inspired, divinely written, and a living Word from God. Seek his guidance first. What makes it living is that we can apply its principles and promises for our life today.

How we believe "works" for us. You need to find what "works" for you. We are concerned that you become scripturally literate. We don't want you to fall for every wind of doctrine (Eph 4: 12-16):

> "…so that the body of Christ may be built up until we reach unity in the faith and in the knowledge of the Son of God and become mature, attaining to the whole measure of the fullness of Christ. Then we will no longer be infants, tossed back and forth by the waves, and blown here and there by every wind of teaching and by the cunning and craftiness of men in their deceitful scheming. Instead, speaking the truth in love, we will in all things grow up into him who is the Head, that is, Christ. From him the whole body, joined and held together by every supporting ligament, grows and builds itself up in love, as each part does its work."

We need to become a supportive community for each other. We can learn from each other. Those who are a little more mature in their faith need to share their experiences, how their faith has been strengthened, and what scriptures have helped them. We believe we were created for relationship not only with God but with other believers.

We can't give you our faith. It wouldn't help you anyway. Like the parable of the women who didn't take any oil with them (Matthew 25: 1-13), each of us is responsible for his/her own faith.

Pray before you read God's Word. Ask God to open up something in His scripture for your understanding and application. In John's gospel (John 14: 26), Jesus tells his disciples that the Holy Spirit will teach them all things and will remind them of everything he told them. Meditate and study the Bible for the foundation of your belief. Educate yourself. Use commentaries if you have them available to you. Listen with an open mind to those who may be more experienced or learned. Think for yourself and share your faith with confidence knowing it comes from the foundation of scripture. Share in faith tempered with loving each other as Christ loves each of us.

DAY 1: GOD WILL NEVER GIVE YOU MORE THAN YOU CAN HANDLE

Open each day's study with this prayer or one of your own:

"In my distress I called to the Lord;
I cried to my God for help.
From his temple he heard my voice;
my cry came before him, into his ears."

Psalm 18: 6

You know what *they* say, "God will never give you more than you can handle."

Excuse me! If God thinks I can handle this, he thinks too highly of me. Right? We've heard many grieving parents say this. Most of the time, it's more out of resignation than what they truly believe. This is a good example of a religious cliché that is loosely supported in scripture. Any verse taken out of context and not quoted exactly takes on a meaning that isn't correct. It becomes an interpretation of the reader.

Read 1 Corinthians 10: 1-13

Verses 1-12 set the context for verse 13. Paul is saying that the Israelites had fallen into temptation and sin. He says, "Do not be idolaters, as some of them were; as it is written: 'The people sat down to eat and drink and got up to indulge in pagan revelry.' We should not commit sexual immorality, as some of them did—and in one day twenty-three thousand of them died. We should not test the Lord, as some of them did—and were killed by snakes. And do not grumble, as some of them did—and were killed by the destroying angel."

Verse 11 (NIV) Please fill in the blanks:

These things happened to them as _____ and were written down as _____ for us, on whom the fulfillment of the ages has come.

1. What do we need to be careful not to do?

We need to be careful not to fall into temptation or from setting our hearts on evil things.

Verse 12 (NIV) Please fill in the blanks:

So, if you think you are _____ _____, be careful that you _____

_____.

Verse 13 (NIV) Please fill in the blanks:

No _____ has seized you except what is _____ to man. And God is

faithful; he will not _____ you be _____ beyond _____ _____

_____ _____. But when you are _____, he will also

_____ a way out so that you can _____ _____ under it.

Read James 1: 13

Read Matthew 4: 1-11

2. Who is the tempter?

Matthew 4:1 describes the tempter as the devil. James 1:13 assures us that God tempts no one. God is not the *giver* in 1 Corinthians 10: 13 of temptation. He is the provider of the way out or the ability to resist that temptation if we ask for it in prayer

3. What happens in Matthew 4: 11?

After Jesus resists temptation, the devil leaves him alone. Then the angels came and attended him. Jesus was led by the Spirit into the desert to be tempted by the devil. After fasting 40 days and 40 nights he was hungry. The tempter (devil) began testing him. Jesus' ability to resist temptation came from fasting and prayer.

Read Matthew 26: 53

Read Luke 22: 43

4. Can we call on God for strength and courage to resist temptation?

Of course we can! God is faithful.

5. Does 1 Corinthians 10: 13 or any other scripture support that God will never give us more than we can handle? What do you believe in relation to applying this verse to your grief?

Day 2: They Were Ready to Go

Opening Prayer:

"In my distress I called to the Lord;
I cried to my God for help.
From his temple he heard my voice;
my cry came before him, into his ears."

Psalm 18: 6

We had lived in a small town in northern Missouri up until the day of Craig's accident. There were four young men in the car involved. Craig was a passenger seated behind the driver. The driver and Craig were killed instantly in a very violent single car roll over. Two of the young men were seriously hurt but ultimately survived and are doing well. None were wearing seat belts.

All four were eighteen years old and had graduated from high school six weeks before the accident. The two who died went to church regularly. The two who survived didn't go to church.

The word about town was that God took the two who were "ready to go" and left the two so that they could get "ready".

1. What is your opinion of this word about town?

2. What message does this give young people?

The message this sends to young people is don't be ready, or God will take you out. What was really unfortunate about this rumor is that we knew all of these young men. One of the survivors was Craig's best friend. They had plans to be roommates at college in the fall. Even though he didn't go to church nor did he live what might be considered by some as a Christian lifestyle, he was a believer.

We are extremely grateful that Craig had professed his faith in Jesus. We have the assurance that Craig is in heaven. Although it is vitally important that children learn about Jesus and his love, there are unbelievers who die every day. There are also believers who die every day. It's important to be "ready".

Read Matthew 25: 1-13

3. What is the lesson of this parable?

In a nutshell—be ready. In verse 12 Jesus says, "I tell you the truth. I don't know you. Therefore, keep watch, because you do not know the day or the hour." Preparedness for Christ's return cannot be shared or transferred. Being ready to meet Christ is not being selfish or uncaring.

Read Acts 15: 6-11

Verse 15:8 (NIV) Please fill in the blanks:

God, who knows the _____, showed that he _____ _____ by giving the _____ _____to them, just as he did to us.

Only God knows the heart. We don't know the conversations that anyone has with God. As humans, we lack the perfect knowledge about one another, and we lack impartiality to make such decisions. Our humanness does not allow us the right to decide or even offer an opinion about a person's eternity.

Read Matthew 7: 1-5
> **Luke 16: 15**
> **Psalm 94: 11**

Read Matthew 20: 1-16

Verse 12 (NIV) Please fill in the blanks:

"These who were hired _____ worked _____ _____ _____,' they said 'and you have made them _____ to us who have borne the burden of the work and the heat of the day."

Verse 15 (NIV) Please fill in the blanks:

"Don't I have _____ _____ to do what_____ _____ with my own money? Or are you _____ because I am _____?"

4. Is it ever too late to become a believer?

5. Who knows a person's heart and thoughts?

DAY 3: GOD WORKS IN MYSTERIOUS WAYS

Opening Prayer:

"In my distress I called to the Lord;
I cried to my God for help.
From his temple he heard my voice;
my cry came before him, into his ears."

Psalm 18: 6

Over the years, we have been involved in many funeral services. We've heard it said many times by well-meaning people who perhaps simply want to bring comfort but don't know what to say.

God works in mysterious ways. What does that mean? Certainly, God sees a bigger picture than we do. His ways are too wonderful for us to know.

For the grieving family, it must mean that the ways of God can't be known but can be trusted.

Read Isaiah 55: 8-9

1. What does this scripture mean for you?

Read Job 11: 7-8

2. Do you trust in the mysteries of God?

Read Job 42: 1-3

Job realizes that God's purposes are supreme. How do you understand the supremacy of God?

Read 1 Corinthians 13: 1-7

We learn from 1 John 4: 8 that God is love. Therefore, we can insert God in place of love in this scripture. Verse 4 becomes God is patient, God is kind…

3. What do you believe the character of God to be?

DAY 4: A MERRY HEART

Opening Prayer:

"In my distress I called to the Lord;
I cried to my God for help.
From his temple he heard my voice;
my cry came before him, into his ears."

Psalm 18: 6

I (Elaine) could tell she was on a mission when I first caught sight of her coming through the door. She marched over to me with a determined look on her face. She pinned something on my dress while saying, "I have something for you."

It was May, and the church was having a fellowship meal honoring our graduates. Craig had died six weeks after he graduated from high school. I felt obligated to be there because of my roll as pastor's wife. I wanted to be supportive of David, and I really did want to be supportive of our graduates. However, it had been less than a year since Craig died. I was struggling for composure and an attitude of congratulations. I had put on the phony smile I reserved for such occasions.

I was not greeted warmly by the woman. There was no smile, phony or otherwise, on her face. No hug.

I looked down at what she had pinned on my dress. It was homemade. It was kind of pretty. It had something written on it that I couldn't read upside down. I retreated to the restroom to read what it said.

Read Proverbs 17: 22

A homemade heart with this verse of scripture attached was what she pinned to my dress. It felt like she was judging me. I thought I was doing well. I was there. I had a pretty dress on. I had fixed my hair and put on makeup minus mascara—just in case I started to cry. I couldn't muster a cheerful heart.

1. How do you handle the expectations of others?

It's a part of grief work to do those things that help us move forward. However, we can't pretend our way through. A cheerful heart is good medicine but it's simply that—medicine. It takes time and work to heal. Be gentle with yourself. Don't allow others to steal what they have no right to take—your right to mourn. Grief is the price we pay for loving our child. Denying our pain will put us in danger of stuffing it or getting stuck. Moving forward is a decision we make to not let the pain defeat us and drive us to unhealthy behaviors. It hurts. It's normal to grieve.

2. Share with God all of the hurtful things others have said.

DAY 5: REAL CHRISTIANS DON'T CRY

Opening Prayer:

"In my distress I called to the Lord;
I cried to my God for help.
From his temple he heard my voice;
my cry came before him, into his ears."

Psalm 18: 6

If we are confident that our loved one had accepted Jesus before they died, some people believe that any expression of grief defies that confidence. If our loved one is in heaven, we should be happy and not sad.

There are many versions of stories or poems that have been read at funerals that admonish grief. They usually pretend to be written by the person who has died. They are some rendition of, "Don't stand by my grave and weep." Crying, especially by men, is seen as a sign of weakness. Crying in grief is seen by some people as weakness of faith.

Read John 11: 33-36

Verse 33 (NIV) Please fill in the blanks:

When Jesus saw her _____, and the Jews who had come along with her also

_____, he was _____ _____in spirit and

_____. "Where have you laid him?" he asked. "Come and see, Lord," they replied.

Verse 34 (NIV) Fill in the blanks:

_____ _____.

Verse 36 (NIV) Please fill in the blanks:

Then the Jews said, "See how he _____ _____!"

John 11 is the story about Jesus and the death of his friend Lazarus. Jesus wept because he loved him. We cry because we loved and still love our child. Period!

1. Do you believe crying is a weakness? Do you have a tendency to "stuff" your feelings? Do you think you are grieving in a healthy way?

Read John 14: 26

The KJV reads:

"But the Comforter, which is the Holy Ghost, whom the Father will send in my name, he shall teach you all things, and bring all things to your remembrance, whatsoever I have said unto you."

We desire a life that is trouble free—one that doesn't need a Comforter. That's not reality.

Read Matthew 5:4
   Isaiah 61: 1-3
   Luke 4: 16-19

Jesus came to fulfill this scripture. He came to comfort all who mourn, and provide for those who grieve—to bestow on them a crown of beauty instead of ashes, the oil of gladness instead of mourning, and a garment of praise instead of a spirit of despair.

2. Do you believe it is wrong for a Christian to grieve or cry?

Read 1 Thessalonians 4: 13-18

Verse 13 (NIV) Please fill in the blanks:

Brothers, we do not want you to be ignorant about those who fall asleep, or to _____ like the rest of

men, who _____ _____ _____.

3. What is the hope you are holding on to?

God Wouldn't Let Me Go — by Elaine

I'll be the first to admit that I was a mess for the first few *years* after Craig's death. I was terrified of losing my faith. I didn't want much to do with God or a relationship with Him. I was also afraid not to have a relationship with God. To say I was confused is an understatement of huge proportion. I wanted to believe in God but I didn't know how to get there. I really didn't think I could. What tormented me was—*What if there really is a God and I turned my back on Him?*

I had been watching Joyce Meyer on TV every day for about a year prior to Craig's death. At that time, she ended every program saying, "There's Life in the Word." Her ministry was titled *Life in the Word.*

After Craig died, I continued to watch mostly out of habit. Every day she made me mad. I'd think, well you'd change your tune if you lost a child. Every time I thought a positive thought about God it felt like I was letting Him off the hook. Finally, one day I opened my Bible and said, "God, if there is life in here, You'll have to show me." I opened my Bible and God began revealing Himself to me. Not all at once, but slowly and gently. He started whispering truth to me as I read. I resisted at first but in time I allowed Him to minister to my wounded heart.

For at least two years after Craig died, I slept an average of two or three hours a night. My mind wouldn't shut down. I had to figure it all out. I was exhausted but couldn't sleep. I was miserable. I honestly thought I was going crazy. I also thought I could very easily be destined for hell for my unbelief. Maybe I was living hell on earth. I devoured books. I read every book I could find—especially by other bereaved parents. I also wrote poetry. It seemed to help organize my thoughts.

There were two books that helped me tremendously. *A Grace Disguised* by Gerald Sittser and *Lament for a Son* by Nicholas Wolterstorff. Both of these men are religious teachers **and** fathers who have lost children.

Even when I wanted to run, God was there. He put so many people, books, scripture readings, and sermons in my path to guide me back to Him. I am so grateful that God wouldn't let me go. He held me when I didn't know where to turn. He patiently waited for me to turn to Him. Then He gave me all the understanding and grace I need to trust Him and His love. There is life in the Word.

I wrote the following poems in my time of torment.

A Merry Heart

Maybe it was simply an innocent gesture.
She couldn't know the timing just wasn't right.
I could tell she was a woman on a mission,
when we first caught each other's sight.

She politely said, "I have something to give you."
I thought to myself, "Oh great, more advice."
I watched her pin something on my dress.
It looked kind of pretty. I responded, "How nice."

It had a pretty heart and ribbon,
and possibly a quotation from a book.
It was impossible to read upside down.
So I scurried off to take a private look.

A merry heart doeth good like medicine.
From the Book of Proverbs 17: 22.
Proverbs are intended as words to live by,
Words of encouragement for me and you.

I was right from the beginning!
There it was, more advice!
I felt a rage well up inside me,
and what I was thinking wasn't nice.

God, can I reach out and grab her?
Maybe slap her once or twice?
For I thought her to be self-righteous
I certainly didn't need **her** advice.

I wanted to pick her up and shake her!
Hard! Until her teeth rattled!
She knew nothing about my struggle,
what I feared and what I battled.

I thought I was doing a miraculous job,
just to keep my tears in check.
We were there for a celebration,
And my son had died in a car wreck.

Sure it happened almost a year ago,
but our celebration was for graduation,
for the present year's class and families,
the first anniversary of Craig's graduation.

Give me credit for at least putting clothes on,
fixing my hair and spraying on nice perfume.
I'll never apologize for any tear I've shed,
or what she perceives as gloom and doom.

If a man has both legs amputated,
would she say, "It's time to walk again."
I feel like a person with a shattered heart,
being told, "It's time to laugh again."

If she is asking me to get over it,
or to put a smile on my face—I can't.
It will take a little more than medicine.
I'm waiting for a heart transplant.

That will take some divine intervention.
I understand I can't do it on my own.
She probably just wanted to make it better.
This is something God and I must do alone.

•••

To Whom It May Concern

It has been eighteen months.
It's time to get over *it*.
What is *it* **you** need for **me** to get over?
Is *it* time?
Is *it* a thing I can leap over?
Is *it* grief?
Is *it* love?
I've seen other parents go through *it*.
I've seen *it* let them laugh again.
Maybe *it* is hope.
If you don't want to help me through *it*,
At least don't judge *it*.
Someday I trust I'll see it differently.
But for now *it* is my son, Craig.

•••

Testing of Experience — by David

"Truth is what stands the test of experience."
Albert Einstein

So many actual words. From the very beginning, I was bombarded by words. "Craig's dead." Tears and sobs followed.

Gene and Linda Shaw told a pastor acquaintance of theirs in California about us and our loss. He was gracious enough to send us a letter in which he warned me about some of the people I would meet. He said, "Give them a break. They don't know what they are talking about."

I received many phone calls from unexpected and expected people. I don't even remember what any of them said. I do, however, remember that some were genuine surprises and overwhelming in their gentleness and support.

Several months into the grief, I remember a kind woman in our congregation asking me in all sincerity, "Aren't you over it yet?" Out of respect for her, I stifled an angry reply.

After a few months of attending the Mid-Missouri chapter of TCF meetings, I recall being comforted by the other grieving parent's words and sometimes simply their presence. I continue to be lifted up by our friends of the Four-States chapter of TCF.

I would often say words to myself. Sometimes they were words of recrimination or confusion, and at other times they were words of affirmation. I would ask myself why I didn't have Craig move with us. "Craig, where are you? Where is heaven? Are you behind that full moon or are you beside me," I'd ask? Most often I would simply say, "I love you, Son."

Then, there were the times when I just didn't have the words to express myself. Times when God had to fill in the gaps of sighs too deep for words.

Eventually, words became a source of encouragement. Both Elaine and I devoured books on grief and grieving. I tried hard to make sense out of this world I had been pushed into.

Elaine became so creative with her writings that I would just be quiet and let her sometimes gentle and sometimes raw words sink inside myself.

Everything that was said or written became filtered through the lens of Craig's absence. Songs on the radio had different meanings than before. I would see crosses and flowers at different points along the highway and remember Craig's memorial that his friends left beside the accident site in Braymer.

Most of the words spoken to us that I have found less than helpful were spoken out of ignorance. Thank God most people don't understand the depth of pain that comes from having a child die. But then there have been some along the way who have just been hateful and mean. Thankfully, these people have been very few but they are also the ones I vividly remember. After much thought and reflection, I now realize that sinning in speech reflects sin in spirit. As the pastor mentioned earlier advised me, "Give them a break. They don't know what they are talking about."

Words can cut. They can comfort. There are times when words are all I have to express my love for Craig, Elaine, and all my family.

❦

Week Five

WRESTLING WITH GOD

WEEK FIVE
WRESTLING WITH GOD

There comes a time when we simply must take all of our questions, confusion, anger, fears, and pain to God and wrestle it all out with Him. Trying to hide behind a phony façade for the sake of others isn't healthy for us. We aren't fooling anyone but ourselves if we try to fake our faith. It becomes a heavy burden that we don't need to bear.

It's very liberating to release all of our pent up feelings and heap them on God until He addresses each of them. We may not like the process but we will like the results. Living free of doubt, unbelief, and a broken relationship with God is living in peace beyond understanding and true joyful living.

The Bible has some examples of people who have wrestled with God and emerged as warriors of faith. God can handle us shaking our fist and hurling angry words at Him. Be prepared. Job challenged God to come down and explain Himself. God did just that and Job was left with answers to questions he didn't even know he had. God is faithful. Job said, "Surely I spoke of things too wonderful for me to know (Job 42: 3)." We will spend next week with Job.

It's not wrong to have questions or even anger toward God. He understands our pain, our suffering. It's wrong to stay angry. We believe God expects us to turn to Him with everything including our doubts. How else can we grow beyond a very superficial faith? If we never have need of Him, we will never seek Him with our whole heart. He wants us to draw near to Him and to allow Him to speak for Himself.

Wrestling with God takes tremendous courage. It means coming out into the open and standing naked before God. We wouldn't recommend doing it if we weren't certain that God loves each of us and desires to show each of us just how much. He wants to be in relationship with you as much as you want, and need, to be in relationship with Him. He already knows our deepest thoughts and broken heart. He knows the thoughts we haven't shared with anyone. We aren't going to surprise Him with how we feel.

God will still be God whether we acknowledge Him or not.

It's for our own sake and benefit that we wrestle it out with God.

DAY 1: JACOB

Open each day's study with this prayer or one of your own:

"Creating God, I thank you that my strength comes from you.
I know that you guard me when I leave you and when I return.
Preserve me through your mighty presence."

Amen

Jacob was twin brother to Esau. They were the sons of Isaac and grandsons of Abraham.

> The boys grew up, and Esau became a skillful hunter, a man of the open country, while Jacob was a quiet man, staying among the tents. Isaac, who had a taste for wild game, loved Esau, but (his wife) Rebekah loved Jacob.
> Once when Jacob was cooking some stew, Esau came in from the open country, famished. He said to Jacob, "Quick, let me have some of that red stew! I am famished!" (That is why he was also called Edom.)
> Jacob replied, "First sell me your birthright."
> "Look, I am about to die," Esau said, "What good is the birthright to me?"
> But Jacob said, "Swear to me first." So he swore on oath to him, selling his birthright to Jacob.
> Then Jacob gave Esau some bread and some lentil stew. He ate and drank, and then got up and left.
> So Esau despised his birthright. (Genesis 25: 27-34)

In ancient times the birthright included the inheritance rights of the firstborn (Heb 12: 16). Jacob was ever the schemer, seeking by any means to gain advantage over others. But it was by God's appointment and care, not Jacob's wits, that he came into the blessing.[11]

In ancient times a verbal oath was all that was required to make the transaction legal and forever binding.[12]

Read Genesis 27: 1-40

Verse 27 (NIV)

> "Ah, the smell of my son is like the smell of a field that the Lord had blessed.
> May God give you of heaven's dew and of earth's richness—an abundance of grain and new wine.
> May nations serve you and peoples bow down to you. Be lord over your brothers, and may the sons of your mother bow down to you. May those who curse you be cursed and those who bless you be blessed.

---

[11]NIV text note page 45, *The NIV Study Bible*, Copyright 1985, 1995, 2002 by the Zondervan Corporation
[12]ibid

Jacob had stolen Esau's birthright, and now, he has stolen Esau's blessing. Again, a verbal blessing was considered to be legal and binding.

As a result of Jacob's scheming Esau was furious and vowed to kill Jacob. Jacob was forced to leave in fear of his life.

Jacob went to live with his mother's brother, Labon. He settled in Horan where he took wives and had 12 children (creating the 12 tribes of Israel).

After many years away from his homeland, Jacob decided to return. This meant that he would have to face his brother Esau.

Read Genesis 32: 1-21

1. How did Jacob prepare to meet his brother Esau?

Jacob sent messengers ahead to present gifts to Esau to perhaps pacify him so that he might receive Jacob and not kill all of them.

Read Genesis 32: 22-32

Verse 24 (NIV) Please fill in the blanks:

So Jacob was left _____, and a man _____ with him till

_____.

2. *With whom did Jacob wrestle and why?*

We'll discover later that he wrestled with God. Jacob was afraid and wanted God's protection but he also knew he really didn't deserve it. He finally realized how wrong he had been and how despicable he had been toward Esau. He had every reason to be afraid.

Verse 26 (NIV) Please fill in the blanks:

Then the man said, "Let me go, for it is daybreak." But Jacob replied, "I will not let you go unless you

_____ me."

Verses 28-29 (NIV) Please fill in the blanks:

Then the man said, "Your name will no longer be called Jacob, but Israel, because you have struggled with

_____ and with _____ and have _____."

Jacob said, "Please tell me your name." But he replied, "Why do you ask my name?" Then he

_____ him there.

Verse 30 (NIV) Please fill in the blanks:

So Jacob called the place Peniel, saying, "It is because I _____ God _____ to

_____, and yet my life was spared."

In ancient times it was believed that you couldn't see the face of God and live (Exodus 33:20). Jacob must have had a powerful encounter with God. His life was spared and because his life was spared after seeing God, his life would be spared in meeting Esau.

Read Genesis 33: 1-11

3. What was Esau's response to his brother Jacob when they finally met? Why was he so forgiving?

Esau ran to meet Jacob and embraced him. He threw his arms around his neck and kissed him. They both wept. (vs. 4)

In verse 9 Esau says that he has plenty. God had blessed Esau as much as Jacob was blessed. Jacob finally realized that it was God blessing him and it changed him. In seeing God, he saw the character of God.

DAY 2: JOSEPH

Opening Prayer:

"Creating God, I thank you that my strength comes from you.
I know that you guard me when I leave you and when I return.
Preserve me through your mighty presence."

Amen

Read Genesis 37: 1-36

Joseph was the favored son of Jacob. His brothers hated him because Jacob (Israel) loved him more than them. They couldn't stand him, in fact. They wanted to get rid of him and they did.

1. What infuriated them to the point that they plotted to kill him?

Joseph had two dreams in which the meaning was that the brothers would bow down to Joseph. Joseph was next to the youngest and was born to Rachael whom Jacob loved more than his first wife Leah. To "bow down" meant that he would hold the position of leadership and stature that typically was given by tradition to the oldest son. The family hierarchy would be out of order. In the second dream, even his mother and father would bow down to him. His brothers became very jealous and angry. Even their father, Jacob, was disturbed when he heard of the dreams.

2. What did the brothers do?

They first plotted to kill him. Reuben (one of the brothers) convinced them not to kill him, but to throw him into a cistern that didn't have any water in it. Reuben was planning to rescue him.

Verses 25-27 (NIV) Please fill in the blanks:

As they sat down to eat their meal, they looked up and saw a caravan of Ishmaelites coming from Gilead.

Their camels were loaded with _____, _____ and _____ and

they were on their way to take them down to Egypt. Judah said to his brothers, "What will we gain if we kill our

brother and cover his blood? Come, let's _____ him to the Ishmaelites and not lay our hands on him;

after all he_____ _____ _____, our own _____ and

_____." His brothers agreed.

Jacob was taken to Egypt and sold to Potiphar, an Egyptian who was one of Pharaoh's officials.

Genesis 39: 2-5 (NIV) Please fill in the blanks:

The _____ was with _____ and he _____,

and he lived in the house of his Egyptian master. When his master saw that the Lord was with him and that

the _____ gave him _____ in _____he did,

_____ found_____ in his eyes and became _____

_____. Potiphar put him in charge of his household, and he entrusted to his care everything he

owned. From the time he put him in charge of his household and of all that he owned, the Lord _____

the household of the Egyptian because of _____.

In the next several chapters, Joseph is thrown in prison, interprets dreams of two fellow prisoners, interprets a dream of Pharaoh's, Pharaoh releases Joseph from prison and puts him back in charge. For seven years there was an abundance of food because the land produced plentifully. Joseph collected all the food produced in those seven years and stored it in the cities. Huge amounts of grain were stored. Then there was a famine in all of the world, but in Egypt there was food. Ultimately, Egypt became the only place to buy food.

Eventually Joseph's brothers went to Egypt to buy food not knowing what had happened to Joseph.

Read Genesis 42: 6-9

Verse 9 (NIV) Please fill in the blanks:

Then he remembered his _____ about them and said to them, "You are spies! You have come to see where our land is unprotected."

Read Genesis 45: 1-15

Verses 4-5 (NIV) Please fill in the blanks:

Then Joseph said to his brothers, "Come close to me." When they had done so, he said, "I am your brother Joseph, the one _____ _____ into Egypt! And now do not be _____ and do not be _____ with yourselves for selling me here, because it was to _____ lives that _____ sent me ahead of you."

Verse 8 (NIV) Please fill in the blanks:

"So then it was not you who _____ me here , but _____.

By this time, Joseph was more than 30 years old. Do you think that Joseph had questioned God between the time of his dreams and the reuniting with his brothers? While in prison Joseph must have wrestled many times with God. Yet, Joseph later understood that his going to Egypt was necessary for the salvation of his family.

3. Why do you think Joseph didn't hold a grudge against his brothers?

Joseph certainly must have questioned God. He didn't hold a grudge because he listened to God for understanding.

Day 3: Ruth

Opening Prayer:

"Creating God, I thank you that my strength comes from you.
I know that you guard me when I leave you and when I return.
Preserve me through your mighty presence."

Amen

We studied some of this story earlier. At that time, we focused on Naomi. Today we are going to try to see the story through Ruth's eyes. Naomi and her husband along with their two sons had traveled to Moab because there was a famine in their land. The two sons married Moabite women—Orpah and Ruth.

Naomi's husband died in Moab. About 10 years later, Naomi's two sons died. Naomi heard that the famine was over in her homeland and prepared to return there.

She tried to persuade her daughters-in-law to stay with their families in Moab. She thought it would be unfair for them to leave their own families for a hopeless future with her.

Read Ruth 1: 11-18

Verse 16 (NIV) Please fill in the blanks:

But Ruth replied, "Don't urge me to leave you or to turn back from you. Where you go I will go, and where you stay I will stay. Your _____ will be my _____ and your

_____ my _____.

This is a classic expression of loyalty and love disclosing Ruth's character. Ruth makes a selfless decision even though it holds no prospect for her except to share in Naomi's desolation. A widow without sons to care for her put Naomi in an extremely vulnerable position. She and Ruth would have to fend for themselves for their basic needs of food and shelter. Ruth was headed for a land where she would be a foreigner among people who would despise her heritage. Fear and despair must have gripped both of them.

1. Why do think Ruth wanted to assume Naomi's God as her God?

At some point, Ruth must have developed a heart for God. She married an Israelite. They could have been married as many as ten years. She was not only going with Naomi, she was also claiming a new identity. She must have had questions like Naomi. A person cannot go through the grief they experienced without questions. She must have had her own struggle with God.

Read Ruth 2: 1-12

Verse 10-11 (NIV) Please fill in the blanks:

At this she bowed down with her _____ to the _____. She exclaimed, "Why have I found such _____ in you eyes that you notice me—a _____?"

Boaz replied, "I've been told all about what you have done for your mother-in-law since the death of your husband how you _____ your _____ and _____ and your _____ and came to live with people you did not know before.

Read Ruth 2: 17-23

Verse 20 (NIV) Please fill in the blanks:

"The Lord bless him!" Naomi said to her daughter-in-law. "He has not stopped showing his kindness to the living and the dead." She added, "That man is our close _____, he is one of our

_____ _____.

Boaz was a close relative of Ruth's former husband, Mahlon. The closest male relative had the primary responsibility to marry a widow. However, there was a closer male relative than Boaz. Boaz was willing to "redeem" Ruth but he wanted to offer the nearest relative the right first. The kinsman-redeemer was responsible for protecting the interests of needy members of the extended family. This could be accomplished by providing an heir for a brother who had died, to redeem the land that a poor relative had sold outside the family, to redeem a relative who had been sold into slavery, or avenge the killing of a relative. In this case, Boaz marries Ruth and gives her an heir. Ruth's firstborn son would keep Mahlon's name alive and retain ownership of the family inheritance.

Read Ruth 4: 9-17

Ruth and Boaz have a son and name him Obed. Obed was the father of Jesse, the father of King David.

Verse 14 (NIV) Please fill in the blanks:

The women said to Naomi: "Praise be to the Lord, who this day has not left you without a kinsman-redeemer. May

he become _____ throughout _____!

Ruth made a momentous decision to leave her father, mother, and homeland to take care of Naomi. She was willing to marry Boaz to redeem her former husband's family inheritance and to keep his name alive. She had a son who became an heir in place of Mahlon for Naomi. Ruth's self-less love for Naomi proved her to be a woman of noble character (Ruth 3:11).

Naomi transformed from despair, hopelessness, and bitterness to happiness through the selfless, God-blessed acts of Boaz and Ruth.

2. Do you still struggle with hopelessness? If so, how?

DAY 4: JONAH

Opening Prayer

"Creating God, I thank you that my strength comes from you.
I know that you guard me when I leave you and when I return.
Preserve me through your mighty presence."

                                        Amen

Jonah ran from God. He ran as far away as ships could sail, only to return to land within the belly of a giant fish. This story reveals a great truth about God. God can use a stubborn and reluctant prophet to bring the truth to the people who need to hear it. In spite of Jonah's reluctance to present God's message to the people of Nineveh, eventually, God's compassion prevailed in that the entire population of Nineveh repents and experiences God's healing love.

Read Jonah

Verse 1: 1-2 (NIV) Please fill in the blanks:

The word of the Lord came to Jonah son of Amittai; "Go to the great city of Nineveh and _____

against it, because its _____ has come up before me."

Jonah, a prophet, was told by God to go to Nineveh to warn the people to turn from their wicked ways. In this narrative, the people of Israel are to see themselves as in a mirror: their unique position of privilege as the people to whom God had revealed himself in a special way, their stubborn resistance to fulfilling that vocation, and the reason Israel must die as a nation (the judgment the prophets were announcing) and be raised up again refined and renewed (the more distant future the prophets were envisioning)."[13]

Verse 1: 3 (NIV) Please fill in the blanks:

But Jonah _____ _____ from the Lord and headed for Tarshish.

---

[13]Study notes, *The NIV Study Bible*, © 1985, 1995, 2002 by the Zondervan Corporation, pg. 1390

Verse 1: 4 (NIV) Please fill in the blanks:

Then the Lord sent a _____ _____ on the sea, and such a violent

_____ arose that the ship threatened to break up.

The sea in ancient times represented chaos. The sea was threatening. The people understood that God had control of the wind and storms. When the storm came up they each prayed to their god. When they determined that Jonah must be the reason for the calamity, they asked him to pray to his God.

Verse 1: 14-15 (NIV) Please fill in the blanks:

Then they cried to the Lord, "O Lord, please do not let us die for taking this man's life. Do not hold us accountable for killing an innocent man, for you O Lord, have done as you pleased," Then they took Jonah and _____

_____ _____ and the raging _____grew

_____.

The men on the ship knew that God had caused and calmed the storm.   In acknowledgment of His power they offered a sacrifice to Him and made vows to Him. In verse 17 the Lord provided a great fish to swallow Jonah, and Jonah was inside the fish for three days and three nights.

Jonah's prayer in chapter two is a psalm of thanksgiving for deliverance from death in the sea. Jonah knew he deserved death but that God had shown him extraordinary mercy.[14]

Jonah then goes to Nineveh and obeys God's command to preach against their wickedness. Jonah told the people that in 40 days they would be destroyed. The people repented from their wickedness and God showed them mercy and compassion.

Jonah became angry with God for showing compassion to an enemy of Israel. He wanted God's goodness only to be shown to the Israelites and not to the Gentiles.

Verse 4: 2 (NIV) Please fill in the blanks:

He prayed to the Lord, "O Lord, is this not what I said when I was still at home? That is why I was so

---

[14]Ibid pg. 1391

quick to flee to Tarshish. I knew that you are a _____ and _____God

slow to _____ and _____ in _____, a God who

_____ from sending calamity."

1. How did Jonah wrestle with God? How did God show mercy, compassion, and abounding love to Jonah?

Jonah didn't want to do what God had asked him to do. He didn't want God to show mercy to Gentiles. Jonah knew the character of God so he tried to run from Him. The first thing God did was to give Jonah a mirror. He asked him the question, "Do you have a right to be angry?" God showed Jonah compassion, mercy, and abounding love in saving Jonah from himself. He saved Jonah from his jealousy, disobedience, and prejudice.

2. If God handed you a mirror, what question would he ask of you?

Day 5: Elijah

Opening Prayer:

"Creating God, I thank you that my strength comes from you.
I know that you guard me when I leave you and when I return.
Preserve me through your mighty presence."

Amen

Read 1 Kings 17: 1

From the commentary notes in the NIV Study Bible for this verse, we learn that Elijah's name means "the Lord is my God".[15] Elijah was sent as a prophet to vigorously oppose, by word and action, the worship of Baal in the northern kingdom of Israel. Their king, Ahab, had elevated the worship of Baal to an official status. God pronounced divine judgment on the land by sending a drought. Neither dew nor rain would fall as a demonstration that even though Baal was considered the god of fertility and the lord of the rain clouds, he was powerless to give rain.

Read 1 Kings 17: 2-6

1. How did God provide for Elijah during the drought?

The ravens brought him bread and meat twice a day and he drank from the brook.

Read 1 Kings 18: 16-46

Verse 44 (NIV) Please fill in the blanks:

The seventh time the servant reported, "A cloud as small as a man's hand is _____ from the

_____."

---

[15]Ibid pg. 509

2. When we studied about the glimpses of heaven, we learned from Revelation that we are promised that the sea (chaos) would be no more. What significance do you think might be placed on the detail that the cloud raised from the sea?

Read 1 Kings 19: 1-18

Verses 4-5 (NIV) Please fill in the blanks:

…while he himself went a day's journey into the desert. He came to a broom tree, sat down under it, and prayed that he might die. "I _____ _____ _____, Lord," he said, "_____ my _____; I am no better than my ancestors."

3. Why had Elijah given up?

Elijah had lost confidence in the triumph of the kingdom of God and was resigned to quit. He didn't think restoration was possible. He lost sight of God's ability to redeem Israel and provide for Elijah.

Read 1 Kings 19: 9-18

Verse 9 (NIV) Please fill in the blanks:

There he went into a cave and spent the night. And the word of the Lord came to him: "What are

_____ _____ _____, Elijah?"

4. What is your struggle or how are you wrestling with God? Is your struggle in the past? What did you learn?

My Wrestle with God — by Elaine

It's horrid to lose a child. As a writer, I struggle with a word or even a group of words beyond horrid, awful, tormenting, debilitating, or devastating to describe the pain that is grief. There is a reason why losing a child is said to be a parent's worst nightmare. Only, it doesn't last a night, week, or year. It's for the rest of our lives.

Emotional, mental, physical, and spiritual pain took me to a place where I wanted to escape. It gripped me. It held me in sheer torment. I didn't want to live, die, think, read, pray, or get out of bed. It became a very conscious choice for me to get up, put clothes on, and face the day. My first thought of the day was, Craig's dead. My last thought of the day and every thought between was, Craig's dead. How in the world am I going to survive—to live the rest of my life with a shattered heart?

I wasn't a mother to my surviving children. I wasn't a wife to my husband. I didn't function in any relationship, including my relationship with God. Maybe the best word to describe me was a zombie. Alive, barely breathing, but good for nothing. I felt so ugly. I would have given anything to shut my mind off for even five minutes. I thought about it and thought about it and thought about it…… I'm not sure I didn't contemplate suicide. I thought about and possibly desired falling asleep and not waking up simply to escape the pain and torment. I used the drugs of food and shopping. I bought things I didn't need if they even remotely reminded me of Craig. I finally realized it didn't help. I really believe I was crazy. I was scary. I scared my family and all those who love me. I even scared myself.

Instinctively I wanted release. I wanted different. I wanted to live again. I only slept two or three hours a night and yet I didn't rest. I was exhausted—spent—at 50 years old. I went through the motions of life but I didn't participate in it. I tried. Only a bereaved parent isn't gagging by now. Most people would judge—DRAMA QUEEN.

My behavior wasn't a show to gain attention or sympathy. It was brutally real. In desperation I reached out. I saw a counselor. I talked to whomever would listen. I wore some people out, especially David, with my constant talking about *it*. I didn't quit *trying* to participate in life. My grandson was born 2 years after Craig died. I wanted so much to simply enjoy being grandma again (I also have a precious granddaughter). I wanted to laugh again—belly busting laugh again. The love was there for my grandson, Luc. The same love I had and still have for Craig is there for my kids and grandkids, David, family, and friends. Love never ends!

The human heart is resilient. We are wonderfully and fearfully made (Psalm 139). The same God-designed endocrine system that sets the physiology of grief in motion is the same endocrine system that God uses to bring about healing.

It wasn't only the "Craig's dead" thoughts that tormented me, it was the "WHY?!!!" thoughts that locked me in a prison of fear, terror, and unbelief. How could a loving God do this do me? I reasoned that if He didn't do this, He allowed it happen. How could He! How could He!

In my lamenting one day, God said, "Exactly!" What's that supposed to mean? "I didn't do this to you and I do love you," God said. That moment set into motion my "wrestle" with God that lasted at least a couple of years. Every time I would begin to accept God's love again it felt like I was betraying my love for Craig. God held me in His loving arms, all the while I was kicking and screaming and beating Him on the chest. Thank You God for not letting me go!

God took my lament of soul and listened, understood, and then cried with me. The shortest verse of the Bible is—Jesus wept. He cried when he saw Mary and Martha grieving for their brother, Lazarus.

God began opening my eyes to see the wisdom in His written Word, His Word made flesh in His Son, Jesus, and that the Word made flesh is God with us.

I've been transformed by the renewing of my mind. I have peace beyond understanding and a joy overflowing in my soul. This transformation doesn't betray Craig nor does the understanding and joy take his place in my heart. I didn't have to push Craig out of my heart to let joy return. There is now room in my heart to honor the love that can never be separated from me for all my children and grandchildren, including Craig, and to treasure my precious memories of Craig. The essence of Craig is still a part of me. I no longer feel like I'm choosing my surviving children over Craig. My love is unconditional and never-ending. It's a mother's love. It's a beautiful thing I treasure beyond what my children and grandchildren will ever know. Sometimes it's beyond what I can know or comprehend.

•••

What Am I Doing — by David

The premise of this Bible study emerges out of our personal story and that of many of our new friends in grief. As a pastor, I knew there would be emotional turmoil and physical consequences to grief. Oddly, I never appreciated how much of a spiritual journey grief would become for Elaine and me.

It was overwhelming to have to find the strength to put my life back in order after Craig's death and yet there was more required of me for real resolution to take place. I had to wrestle with God.

I asked myself, "Does my discipleship really mean anything?"

I remember hearing a story about the French mathematician Descartes. After he had finished his formal education, he decided that most of what he had been taught was wrong. Now he needed to figure out which parts were true and which were not. The story goes that he began this process by trying to decide if he, Descartes, actually existed. After all, if he didn't exist, then there wasn't much point in figuring out anything else. It was while he was pondering this question that he became aware that he was thinking. His conclusion is remembered by many. He resolved, "I think, therefore I am." First problem solved.

The Friday following Craig's funeral on Monday, I had to make my first pastoral visit. A man in my parish was dying so I mustered all the energy I could and went to the hospital. As I was driving home, it occurred to me that I had not spent any time with God during the past week. I decided that I could at least pray while traveling home. My prayer went something like this, "Dear God. I ask that you be with my boys and girls to protect and guide them…" I stopped in mid sentence. "What the hell am I doing," I asked myself? "Why am I asking God to protect Aaron, Bryon, Catie, and Emma when it was obvious God can't or won't protect anyone?" I was furious. I yelled at God.

I knew then, in that car on Highway 50 west of Jefferson City, Missouri, that my relationship with God was dramatically and maybe permanently altered. I knew then that I would have to begin to reconstruct - if I could - my faith.

I don't remember the sequence of this journey. I remember being at times angry and at other times profoundly hurt. I remember wondering if it were true that cursing God would result in death. Often, I was simply overwhelmed with exhaustion.

Once in seminary, an instructor asked each of us in the class to share what was our favorite book of the Bible and why it was our favorite. I shared that my two favorite books were Jeremiah and Galatians. Even before Craig's death, I found comfort in how both Jeremiah and Paul expressed their true emotions to God. Jeremiah was hurt by the reaction of many of his friends to his prophetic message. He wasn't pious in his prayer life or shy about asking God to strike down the people who had insulted him and caused him pain. The Apostle Paul was brutally honest about his relationships with others and with God in his writings to the Galatian church. I often returned to these examples of courageous faith.

However, they are not the only such examples found in the Bible. I often wonder, "How have we gotten to a place where honest expression is seen as inappropriate?" How in the world is a person closer to God because they use King James English when they pray than someone else who speaks plainly from their heart?

I've learned along the way that while God can handle my anger, I am not supposed to build a house for my pain. God wants me to proceed beyond the visceral reactions to my new normal. I've learned that it is alright to be angry with God but it is not alright to stay angry with God.

I believe that God's presence will be with me if I'm willing to watch and listen for it. What I've just written can be very hard to accomplish but I know that it is worth the effort. Wrestling with God is where many women and men in the scriptures found themselves. What I am doing now is praising God where and when I can. Now I am not afraid to offer an honest question to God. I still believe that there is much in our lives that is mystery and may never be explained. I also believe that many times we don't understand because we don't ask and then stay engaged until God reveals God's self to us.

Week Six

JOB

WEEK SIX
JOB

For many of us, when we think of suffering we immediately think of Job and Jesus. We will study the trials and triumph of Jesus for the final 3 weeks.

This week we will study the book of Job. Last week we studied some people who wrestled with God. Job certainly wrestled with God, also. While we could spend the entire 10 weeks studying the book of Job, we will study some of the key verses that led us to find comfort in this seemingly troublesome book of the Bible.

As a pastor and wife, we are often asked by grieving parents to explain the book of Job. Generally what they are asking without coming out and saying it is why God would subject a child of his to such intense suffering.

We, as grieving parents, believe we can relate to Job's suffering. For no apparent reason of his own, Job lost everything. He lost his wealth, health, and children. Losing one's health and wealth is bad enough but to lose all of one's children seems unbelievably cruel and intolerable. We wonder why God seems so indifferent and uncaring. Without a deeper understanding, God appears overbearing and quite frankly a bully. He inflicts suffering simply because he can—he's the all-powerful ruler of the universe.

Before we lost Craig, we avoided the book of Job. We too had conflicting feelings about God's treatment of this loyal, devoted man. As long as we could live life without dealing with the controversial nature of Job's suffering, we didn't see the need to bring it up. We taught around it, skimmed through it to the fairy-tale ending, or passed it off as the Old Testament. It's so much easier to teach from the New Testament.

However, we soon realized that our lack of understanding was a huge stumbling block for our returning to spiritual health. Job loomed in the back of our minds and our hearts as that piece of the puzzle that simply didn't fit in the picture of a loving God. We had to seek understanding in the book of Job. It was difficult, challenging, and took a very long time.

☒ We were right there with Job when he cursed the day he was born.
We could relate.
☒ We were right there with Job when he lamented that he felt that he had no future and that he had nothing in which to live.
We could relate.
☒ We were right there with Job when he argued with his friends that he was being treated unfairly.
We, too, could relate to the unfairness.

After a lot of work reading and studying, seeking God for understanding through prayer, and finally listening to God, we were right there with Job when he encountered God in such a powerful way that he saw the true character of God. We, too, could relate.

DAY 1: THE CONVERSATION BETWEEN GOD AND SATAN

Open each day's study with this prayer or one of your own:

"Creator God, we ask that you take us up into your loving arms, hold us tenderly, and bless us with your presence. We ask for the gift of peace. Help us to walk all of our days with the knowledge that our times are in your hands."

Amen.

The discourse between God and Satan is where many people get stuck in the book of Job. How could a loving God *seemingly* turn Job over to Satan to do anything he wanted to do?

Read Job 1: 1-5

1. What was Job's character?

He was described by God himself as blameless and upright. He feared (respected) God and shunned evil.

2. What was Job's wealth?

He was very wealthy. Notice that his seven sons and three daughters were listed under his "possessions." He had large numbers of sheep, camels, oxen, donkeys, and servants. He was the richest man in the entire East. In the Old Testament times, wealth was equated with righteousness because it indicated favor from God.

Read Job 1: 6-22

The angels and Satan came to present themselves before God. They came as members of the heavenly council to stand before God. Satan was the accuser. He went about the earth looking for people to accuse of unrighteousness.

Verse 8 (NIV) Please fill in the blanks:

The Lord asks if Satan has noticed Job.

"There is no one on earth like him; he is _____ and _____, a

man who _____ God and _____ _____."

3. What is God's opinion of Job? What does God know about Job?

God sees Job as about as good as a person can get. God knows what Job will do. He doesn't predict what Job will do; he knows the end from the beginning. God knows that there is nothing Satan can do to Job that he can't or won't restore to him.

4. What is Satan's response to verse 8?

Does Job fear God for nothing? You've given him everything he could want. He has the best of circumstances. Why wouldn't he fear (respect) God?

5. What is at the heart of Satan's accusation?

God commends Job for his righteousness. Satan tells God that Job is self-serving. Take away his possessions and Job will curse God to his face. Satan questions Job's heart and his reason for respecting God.

Verse 12 (NIV) Please fill in the blanks:

"The Lord said to Satan, 'Very well, then, everything he _____ is in your hands, but on the

man himself _____ _____ _____ _____

_____.'"

Satan was given the power to afflict but is kept on a leash. Satan is still under God's power. God is in control of his creation.

Read Job 2: 1-10

6. What was Job's second test?

Although Job had remained faithful through the first test, he is tested a second time. This time Satan takes Job's health.

Verse 3 (NIV) Please fill in the blanks:

"And he still maintains his _____, though you incited me against him to ruin him

_____ _____ _____."

Verse 4 (NIV) Please fill in the blank:

"Skin for skin! Satan replied, "A man will give all he _____ for his own life.

So far all that Job has given up are his possessions. His second test involved being afflicted with sores all over his body. His second test involved physical pain, isolation, and rejection.

Verse 6 (NIV) Please fill in the blanks:

"The Lord said to Satan, 'Very well then, he is in your hands. But you must _____

_____ _____.'"

Why does God tell Satan to spare Job's life?

Satan is still under God's control. If Job should die, neither God nor Job could be vindicated.

7. *Was Job aware of the reason for his testing?*

Not really. In verse 10 he says, "You are talking like a foolish woman (his wife), shall we accept good from God, and not trouble?"

8. *Did Job remain faithful?*

Yes. In all this, Job did not **sin** in what he said (verse 10).

9. *Who wanted Job defeated?*

Satan.

DAY 2: JOB'S FRIENDS

Opening Prayer:

"Creator God, we ask that you take us up into your loving arms, hold us tenderly, and bless us with your presence. We ask for the gift of peace. Help us to walk all of our days with the knowledge that our times are in your hands."

Amen.

Job had three friends--Eliphaz, the Temanite; Bildad the Shuhite; and Zophar, the Naamathite. When these friends heard about Job's troubles, they went to him to bring comfort and counsel.

When they arrived and saw Job on his pile of ashes scraping himself with a piece of broken pottery, they hardly recognized him. Job was covered with boils from his head to his toes and was so disfigured that even his friends couldn't recognize him.

His friends became so distraught that they tore their robes and sprinkled ashes on their own heads as a sign of loyalty and love. They sat with Job in silence for seven days as was their tradition and as an expression of sympathy for Job.

Unfortunately, they didn't remain silent. They began the very human exercise of attempting to explain the reason for Job's plight.

Read Eliphaz's explanation in Job 4: 7-11

Verse 8 (NIV) sums up his argument. Please fill in the blanks:

As I have observed, those who plow _____, and those who sow _____

_____ it.

It's very simple for Eliphaz. We get what we deserve. Job was experiencing God's wrath for some evil or sin he had committed. From Eliphaz's position, Job should be thankful for the correction God is giving him. Job should humble himself and God would stop punishing him.

Read Bildad's position in Job 8: 1-22

1. What is Bildad's position?

God cannot be unjust. Therefore, Job and his children must be suffering as a result of sinfulness. In Bildad's view, Job should plead for mercy and repent, and God would restore him to his rightful place.

Read Zophar's speech of "counsel" in Job 11: 1-4

2. How did Zophar counsel Job?

Verse 4 (NIV) Please fill in the blanks:

"You say to God, 'My beliefs are _____ and I am _____ in your sight.'"

Job does claim to be blameless in 9: 21. However, Zophar accuses Job of claiming purity and mocking God. Job never makes the claim of purity, nor does he mock God. Purity suggests perfection.

Read Job 11: 13-20

3. What does Zophar assume to be the cause of Job's problems?

Zophar assumes that Job's problems are rooted in his sin, and that all Job has to do is repent for life to become blessed and happy again.

4. What is the common theme for all three friends?

All three friends suggest that Job's trouble is due to sin and that Job needs to repent. If Job would simply repent, Job would be restored.

Read Job 42: 7-9

5. What did God think of the friends' counsel?

God rebuked them. The three friends claimed to know why Job was suffering. We know from day one that Job's sin was not the cause of his trouble.

6. Do you think Job's friends meant well?

DAY 3: JOB'S DEMANDS OF GOD

Opening Prayer:

"Creator God, we ask that you take us up into your loving arms, hold us tenderly, and bless us with your presence. We ask for the gift of peace. Help us to walk all of our days with the knowledge that our times are in your hands."

Amen.

As bereaved parents, we believe we can relate to Job because of his loss of children and the intense suffering that such a loss causes. Job obviously grieved emotionally, mentally, and physically. He also grieved spiritually.

Read Job 7: 1-21

Job has replied to Eliphaz and now addresses God himself. He has lost his purpose in life. He cries out in desperation to God. From his pain and anguish, he wants to know why this is happening to him. In verse 21 he admits he is a sinner but doesn't understand why God won't forgive him.

Read Job 9: 2-3

Job admits he is not sinless. However, he questions what he has done to deserve the severity of suffering God has placed on him. For the rest of chapter nine and into chapter ten, Job voices his complaint against God. Yet, he doesn't abandon God or curse him.

Verse 10: 1 (NIV) Please fill in the blanks:

"I loathe my very life; therefore I will give free rein to my complaint and speak out in the _____

_____ my_____."

Verse 10: 2 (NIV) Please fill in the blanks:

"I will say to God: Do not condemn me, but tell me what _____ you have against me."

Job wants a "hearing" as in a court of law. If God would come down here, Job could plead his innocence. Job knows in his heart that he doesn't deserve his suffering.

Read Job 13: 20-28

1. What does Job want from God?

He wants relief from suffering and the answer as to why this is happening to him. Job doesn't understand that there might be a higher purpose in his suffering than mere punishment for sin. If God would simply give him a reason, he could defend himself.

Job has no knowledge of the conversation that transpired between God and the accuser.

2. What difference do you believe it would have on Job's mental anguish if he were aware of this conversation?

Read Job 14: 18-22 and Chapter 17

Job is despondent. He feels God has abandoned him. He feels alone in his pain and that no one understands his innocence. In fact, all there is left is pain and deep sorrow. All that remains is death.

Read Job 19: 23-29

Verse 25 (NIV) Please fill in the blank:

"I know that my_____ lives, and that in the end he will stand upon earth."

Job believes that when all is said and done his innocence will be revealed. God will vindicate his faithful servants in the face of all false accusations.

Read Job 21

3. Job's friends have elaborated many times on the fate of the wicked. What is Job's response to the fate of the wicked?

Job insists that experience shows that the wicked don't want to know the ways of God and yet prosper and flourish in all they do. They even consider prayer a useless exercise.

4. How have you wrestled with the unfairness of your child's death?

DAY 4: JOB'S ENCOUNTER WITH GOD

Opening Prayer:

"Creator God, we ask that you take us up into your loving arms, hold us tenderly, and bless us with your presence. We ask for the gift of peace. Help us to walk all of our days with the knowledge that our times are in your hands."

Amen.

Job becomes very frustrated over his inability to get God to tell him what he has against him. It's simply not fair.

Read Job 24: 1-12

1. What does Job describe?

Job describes the terrible injustice in the world.

Read Job 24: 13-17

2. Who causes the suffering in the world through their sin?

The murderer, the adulterer, the robber, and those who make friends with darkness cause the suffering of the world.

Verse 17 (NIV) Please fill in the blanks:

"For all of them, _____ _____ is their morning; they make friends with

_____ _____ of _____.

3. What causes suffering?

A world with sin and those who choose to do evil.

4. Will sin always be a part of this world? Will innocent victims suffer?

Yes and yes!

Read Job 24: 21-24

5. Do the wicked get away with their sin?

Job says that God judges the wicked in his own good time. Wickedness and sin will not prevail. Only God understands the wisdom in human suffering—or better yet, the wisdom of remaining faithful to God even in the face of human suffering.

Read Job 28: 20-23

Verse 20 (NIV) Please fill in the blanks:

Where then does _____ come from? Where does _____

dwell?

Verse 23 (NIV) Please fill in the blank:

_____understands the way to it and he alone knows where it dwells.

Read Job Chapters 38-41

Job gets his encounter with God. God neither indicts Job nor does he say that Job is innocent. He doesn't address the reason for his suffering. God tells Job about the accuser.

6. What did Job learn about the wisdom and goodness of God? What did he learn about the sovereignty of God? What did Job learn about the character of God?

Job came into the presence of God and was changed. God no longer needed to explain himself to Job. Job trusted in God's wisdom and sovereignty. God is in control of his creation. God knows and understands what humans can never know.

Read Job 42: 1-6

Job "sees" that the purposes of God are supreme.

Verse 5 (NIV) Please fill in the blanks:

"My _____ had heard of you but now, my _____ have

_____ you.

Job had an encounter with God that was powerful. He saw the character of God and knew that God could be trusted. He no longer had questions. He knew God had vindicated him and that God cared about his faithfulness and righteousness. God would not have come otherwise.

DAY 5: JOB'S RESTORATION

Opening Prayer:

"Creator God, we ask that you take us up into your loving arms, hold us tenderly, and bless us with your presence. We ask for the gift of peace. Help us to walk all of our days with the knowledge that our times are in your hands."

Amen.

What pained Job the most was God's alienation from him. Robbed of every sign of God's favor, Job refuses to turn against God. Job remains faithful to the end. He faces God with anguish, lack of understanding, anger, and bitter complaints, but he never turns away from God. Job yearns for God. He seeks him for an answer.

1. What was at the heart of Satan's accusation? (Job 1: 10)

Satan points out that Job's righteousness is the result of his great wealth. In effect he says that Job's faith is based on his circumstances.

However, when everything is taken away the real test was that of human reasoning. Job wants to reason matters out with God as an equal. He wants to converse one on one with God. What gets exposed are the limits of all human wisdom and understanding.

Job ultimately learns that God's wisdom is supreme. True Godly wisdom is to reverently love God as he first loves us and to trust in the wise goodness of God even though God's ways are at times past the power of human wisdom to fathom.

2. Was there purpose in Job's suffering?

There is purpose only to the extent that Job remained faithful and ultimately encountered the presence of God in such a way that Job experienced God's love on a personal level. One can't come into the presence of God and remain unchanged.

Read Job 42: 7-16

3. How was Job restored?

His restoration was two-fold. One, his relationship with God was restored. He now has a faith based on the character of God and on God's love.

Secondly, Job's wealth, children, and health are restored. *Everything* Satan attempted to take from Job was given back to him. In the case of Job's wealth, God doubled it. Evil will not prevail.

I Can Relate to Job — by Elaine

I'm not a Biblical scholar. I don't have any formal training in Biblical studies. My understanding of Job was very sketchy before Craig died. I didn't see any need to even read about Job. I could have lived the rest of my life without "dealing" with Job. I could have left Job to those who are considered theologians. I could let them figure out why God included this strange story in the Bible which, in my mind, made God look pretty bad.

I soon realized that the strange story in the book of Job was a huge stumbling block for me. Job stood between my doubt and unbelief and a spiritually healthy relationship with God. If I could have stayed in the New Testament with Jesus, I could have reconciled my faith fairly easily. It's easy for me to see compassion, grace, mercy, and goodness in Jesus. I can sing Jesus loves me without question. Every negative feeling I had was toward God. From what I did know about Job, I believed God was anything but loving, compassionate, or full of mercy. In my mind, God tested Job to watch him squirm and prove his loyalty no matter what. He was aloof and uncaring of Job's pain.

This God I had conjured up in my mind was not someone with whom I even remotely wanted to have a relationship. If Job's plight was what I had to do to prove my loyalty, I didn't want to have anything to do with God. If I could have forgotten all about Him and become an atheist, I would have. My torment became the thought, "What about Craig? If there is no God, there is no heaven. Craig is gone forever." I wanted to believe, but I knew deep inside me I had serious doubts and anger at God.

How could a loving God subject not only Job but his own Son to the most intense and cruel suffering known to man to satisfy his wrath? Who would want to serve a God like that? Here I was a pastor's wife with serious issues concerning God.

I'm so grateful that God wouldn't let me go. He patiently allowed me to hurl insults, angry words of contempt, and many words I now regret saying to Him directly at Him. He understood. He not only wouldn't let me go, He fought for me when I was too weak to fight for myself.

Understanding didn't come easily. I began by reading Job from beginning to end. Then I read it again and again. I read commentaries. I started healing when I began relating to more than Job's suffering. I began relating to Job's encounter with God. One day it was as if God was speaking directly to me when he spoke to Job. I then, too, could say, "Before I knew about God. My ears had heard many sermons but then my eyes were opened to the true character of God." It all began to make sense to me. I realize that my heart was touched by God Himself as I read chapter 42 of Job. I can't explain it, but I pray for others to experience it.

I know God fought for me because the unconditional love I have for Craig and my other children and grandchildren is God's love. God is love (1 John 4: 8). It was that unconditional love that couldn't let me go. It wasn't God who wanted Job or me defeated. It was God who redeemed both of us. He restored my soul. I am very grateful. Craig is safe and in heaven—the paradise of God.

Job — by David

I remember it well. I was attending my very first Compassionate Friends meeting. It was more or less a month since Craig's accident. Elaine and I were sitting in the board of directors meeting room at a hospital in Jefferson City, MO. During introductions, I told the group that I was a pastor. Later in the meeting someone asked me, "What about the book of Job?" I recall thinking that I didn't understand this book before Craig died and I really didn't care about it then. I merely said, "I don't know." For a while that was sufficient for me.

After a couple of years, I thought that I would try to read the book of Job. I think I might have finished two sentences before I gave it up. About a year later, I sensed that God was telling me a couple of things. I felt that I was to read the book of Job and I was to read it with the understanding that Job, like me, was a bereaved parent. This understanding made all the difference in the world.

I read the first two chapters, and I was excited. There was much insight that needed to be worked out, but I began to sense a connection between this strange book and my life. I am still trying to harvest its insights.

I remember thinking about the people in my life who had said inconsiderate things to me, like Job's friends had done to him. I wanted, and sometimes did, scream at God for the injustice of it all. I knew that I didn't deserve anything like this. I wanted to know how God felt.

I have moved from avoiding this Old Testament book to beginning to appreciate it for its depth. I no longer chafe at the sovereignty of God that this book presents, even if it is different than I would like. I still struggle with the picture of God that this book lays out, but I am now willing and able to wrestle with its message.

I've learned to appreciate the story within the story. Job still doesn't give many answers. Why undeserved suffering happens is still an open question. The specific resolution given to Job is certainly personal and private. And yet, this strange book, read by one hurting father about another hurting father, gives me hope.

God gives hope and direction. God will not allow the worst that this world can throw at me to ultimately defeat me. Even when my world seems totally chaotic and incomprehensible, God's order is real even if unseen by me.

Week Seven
PSALM 22

Week Seven
Psalm 22

Psalm 23 is familiar to many people. It is read at many funerals and church services. It is known to bring comfort in times of sorrow or when a reminder of God's peace is needed.

Psalm 22 is the psalm immediately preceding the comforting Psalm 23. It isn't comforting at all. In fact, it's quite the opposite. It begins with the disturbing words that Jesus lamented from the cross. "My God, my God, why have you forsaken me?"

Psalm 22 is the anguished prayer of King David. David was the victim of many vicious enemies over a prolonged period of time. He was a Godly man and yet, at times, felt forsaken or forgotten by God. He feels alone in his suffering.

Throughout Jesus' ministry, he quoted from the Psalms. He knew them by heart, as did many believers of that time. How often do we say, "It's in the Bible—somewhere." Jesus told his disciples before he left them that he would bring to their *remembrance* all that he had taught them.

Again, the words of Jesus from the cross are troubling to many of us when we, too, suffer. We can relate to the feelings of forsakenness, aloneness, and abandonment that we envision Jesus must have felt. We, also, wonder why God would forsake his own Son. If God can forsake his own Son, he certainly will forsake us.

This is the danger of taking verses out of context or applying verses to our own circumstances without wisdom from God. This psalm was written in Old Testament times by David. It was the lament of David.

Having said that, in all probability, Jesus repeated not only the first verse of Psalm 22 from the cross, but the entire Psalm. There are other verses that are recorded in the gospels as words spoken by Jesus from the cross. Therefore, we can assume that he must have repeated the entire Psalm.

When we study this Psalm, as a whole, we will understand that Jesus didn't believe God had forsaken him. The words, "My God, my God, why have you forsaken me?" were a cry for help. God was there, present in his suffering, as only a Father can be. We know that Jesus believed his Father was with him when he committed his spirit to God as his final words.

DAY 1: MY GOD, MY GOD

Open each day's study with this prayer or one of your own:

"I love you, O Lord, my strength.
The Lord is my rock, my fortress
and my deliverer;
my God is my rock, in whom I take refuge.
He is my shield and the horn of
my salvation, my stronghold.
I call to the Lord, who is worthy of praise,
and I am saved from my enemies."

Psalm 18: 1-3

In the case of evil, what is almost always true of the victim? Innocence! Evil preys on the innocent. Evil preys on the weakened, also. When you're down, you can count on Satan to show up.

Read 1 Peter 5: 8-11

Verse 8 (NIV) Please fill in the blanks:

"Be self-controlled and alert. Your enemy the devil prowls around like a _____

_____ looking for someone to _____."

Read Psalm 22: 1

David begins his prayer with a question. He asks God, "Why have you forsaken me?"

1. The word forsaken means to be left destitute or to desert. Have you felt forsaken or abandoned by God? If you have, explain the condition.

Read Matthew 27: 46

2. Whose words are these, and what is the circumstance?

These are the words of Jesus from the cross. No other Psalm fitted so aptly the circumstances of Jesus at his crucifixion.

Read Psalm 10: 1-4
    Job 3: 24-26

Read Psalm 22: 2 (NIV) Please fill in the blanks:

"O, my God, _____ _____ _____ by day, but you _____

_____ _____ by night, and am not silent."

Read Job 19: 7 (NIV) Please fill in the blanks:

"Though _____ _____, 'I've been wronged! I get no response; Though

_____ _____ _____ _____, there is no justice."

Read Psalm 42: 3 (NIV) Please fill in the blanks:

My tears have been my food day and night while men say to me all day long " _____ _____

_____ _____?"

Read Psalm 88: 1-3

Verse 1 (NIV) Please fill in the blanks:

"O Lord, the God who saves me, day and night _____ _____ _____ before you."

Jesus, David, and Job are all innocent and righteous sufferers. All cried out to God. All felt God was silent to them.

3. Do you relate? If so, explain your pain.

DAY 2: YET, THE ISRAELITES TRUSTED

Opening Prayer:

"I love you, O Lord, my strength.
The Lord is my rock, my fortress
and my deliverer;
my God is my rock, in whom I take refuge.
He is my shield and the horn of
my salvation, my stronghold.
I call to the Lord, who is worthy of praise,
and I am saved from my enemies."

Psalm 18: 1-3

Read Psalm 22: 3 (NIV) Please fill in the blanks:

"_____ you are enthroned as the _____ _____; you are the

_____ of Israel."

David has cried out in prayer to God and believes God to be silent to his suffering. Then David recalls all that God has been for Israel. His prayer takes a turn toward comfort from the word "yet".

Read Psalm 71: 22 (NIV) Please fill in the blanks:

"I will _____ you with the harp for your _____, O my God;

I will sing praise to you with the lyre _____ _____ _____

_____ _____."

God is said to be the Holy One of Israel and worthy to be praised. His holiness is understood in terms that suggest a divine presence that is described as awesome, mysterious, or overwhelming. The presence of God changes things that are not naturally holy into holiness.

Read Mark 1: 21-28

Verse 24 (NIV) Please fill in the blanks:

"What do you want with us, Jesus of Nazareth? Have you come to destroy us? I know who you are _____

_____ _____ of God."

1. Who is speaking and how do they recognize Jesus?

Evil spirits or demons are speaking and they recognize Jesus as the Holy One of God.

Read Psalm 148: 14 (NIV) Please fill in the blanks:

"He has raised up for his people a _____, the praise of all his saints, of Israel, the people close

to his heart. Praise the Lord."

God is faithful to raise a horn for his anointed. God has performed many "saving" acts for Israel. God should be praised for the redemption of is people.

Read Psalm 22: 4 (NIV) Please fill in the blanks:

"In you our _____ put their_____ they _____

and you delivered them."

Read Psalm 78: 53

Psalm 107: 6 (NIV) Please fill in the blanks:

Then they _____ _____ to the Lord in their _____ and he

_____ them from their _____.

Read Psalm 22: 5 (NIV) Please fill in the blanks:

"They _____ _____ _____ and were _____ In you they

_____ and _____ _____ _____."

Read Isaiah 25: 9

   Isaiah 26: 3-4

   Isaiah 30: 18

2. What is the common theme in all these verses?

The Israelites put their trust in God, and He always delivered them from their trouble. They trusted and were not disappointed. Even though David felt forsaken by God, he turned to God and his faithfulness.

3. What does it mean for you that God has a long history of delivering his children who trust him?

4. What do you envision Jesus thinking as he said the words of this section from the cross?

DAY 3: DO NOT BE FAR FROM ME

Opening Prayer:

"I love you, O Lord, my strength.
The Lord is my rock, my fortress
and my deliverer;
my God is my rock, in whom I take refuge.
He is my shield and the horn of
my salvation, my stronghold.
I call to the Lord, who is worthy of praise,
and I am saved from my enemies."

Psalm 18: 1-3

Read Psalm 22: 6-8

Verse 7 (NIV) Please fill in the blanks:

All who see me _____me; they hurl_____, shaking their heads;

Verse 8 (NIV) Please fill in the blanks:

He _____ in the Lord; let the Lord _____ him. Let the Lord

_____ him, since he _____ in him.

Read Matthew 27: 39-40

Verse 39 (NIV) Please fill in the blank:

Those who passed by _____ at him, shaking their heads.

Verse 40 (NIV) Please fill in the blanks:

You who are going to destroy the temple and build it in three days, save yourself!

Come down from the cross, if you are the _____ of _____.

Read Matthew 27: 41-44

Verse 43(NIV) Please fill in the blanks:

"He _____in God. Let God _____ him now if he wants him, for he said, 'I am

the _____ of _____.'"

Read Psalm 22: 9-11

Verse 9 (NIV) Please fill in the blanks:

_____ you brought me out of the womb; you made me _____ in you even at

my mother's breast.

Verse 11 (NIV) Please fill in the blanks:

Do not _____ _____ from me, for _____ is near and there is

_____ _____ _____ _____.

Read John 16: 31-32

Verse 32 (NIV) Please fill in the blanks:

_____ I am _____ _____, for my _____ is

_____ me.

Trouble is a lonely place. Many of our friends deserted us when Craig died. Grief changes us. In some ways, we are better. We have different priorities. For some of us, we have traveled to the pit of despair. Our friends and some of our relatives don't know what to say and, therefore, are silent and absent. They don't want to make us cry. When we are together, a huge elephant is in the room. In reality there isn't much they can say or do. For some of us and in many ways, only God can save us. Trust in God. Those friends and relatives who truly love us will be used by God to help pull us out of the pit.

1. *Who has God used to help and encourage you?*

Day 4: Dogs, Lions, Bulls, and the Sword

Opening Prayer:

"I love you, O Lord, my strength.
The Lord is my rock, my fortress
and my deliverer;
my God is my rock, in whom I take refuge.
He is my shield and the horn of
my salvation, my stronghold.
I call to the Lord, who is worthy of praise,
and I am saved from my enemies."

Psalm 18: 1-3

Read Psalm 22: 12-18

David's deep distress is expressed in these verses. He uses four figures to portray the attacks of his enemies. He is able to describe his inner sense of powerlessness under their fierce and vicious attacks.

Verse 12 (NIV) Please fill in the blanks:

Many _____ surround me; strong _____ of Bashon encircle me.

Verse 13 (NIV) Please fill in the blanks:

_____ _____ tearing their prey open their mouths wide against me.

Verse 14 (NIV) Please fill in the blanks:

I am poured out like _____ all my _____ are _____ _____

_____. My _____ has turned to _____.

Read Job 23: 16

Verse Psalm 22: 15 (NIV) Please fill in the blanks:

My _____ is dried up like a potsherd, and my _____ sticks to the

_____ _____ _____ _____, you lay me in the

_____ of _____.

Read Job 7: 21 (NIV) Please fill in the blanks:

Why do you not pardon my offenses and forgive my sins? For I will soon lie down _____

_____ _____; you will search for me, but I will be no more.

Read John 19: 28 (NIV) Please fill in the blanks:

Later, knowing that all was now _____, and so that the _____ would be

fulfilled, Jesus said, "_____ _____ _____."

John may be referring to Psalm 69: 21 when he writes—so that the scriptures might be fulfilled, but he is also referring to Psalm 22.

Verse Psalm 22: 16 (NIV) Please fill in the blanks:

_____ have surrounded me, a _____ of _____

_____ has encircled me. They have _____ my hands and _____

_____.

Read John 19: 34 (NIV) Please fill in the blanks:

Instead, one of the soldiers _____ Jesus' side with a _____, bringing a sudden

flow of blood and water.

Read John 19: 36-37

Verse 37 (NIV) Please fill in the blanks:

And, as another scripture says, "They will look on the one they _____ _____.

Read Rev. 1: 7
     Zec. 12: 10

Verses Psalm 22: 17-18 (NIV) Please fill in the blanks:

I can _____ all my _____; people stare and gloat over me. They

_____ my _____ among them and _____ _____

for my clothing.

Read Matthew 27: 35 (NIV) Please fill in the blanks:

When they had crucified him, they _____ up his _____ by

_____ _____.

Read Luke 23: 35-35
     John 19: 24

1. How do you (or do you) equate the forces of dogs, roaring lions, bulls, or the sword (spear) coming after your soul as you grieve?

DAY 5: HE HAS DONE IT; IT IS FINISHED

Opening Prayer:

"I love you, O Lord, my strength.
The Lord is my rock, my fortress
and my deliverer;
my God is my rock, in whom I take refuge.
He is my shield and the horn of
my salvation, my stronghold.
I call to the Lord, who is worthy of praise,
and I am saved from my enemies."

Psalm 18: 1-3

Read Psalm 22: 19-31

Immediately after David pours his heart out to God in prayer, he acknowledges that God is not far off. God has not abandoned or forsaken him and he realizes that his strength comes from God. Then in reverse order he addresses the four forces that had attacked his soul.

Verse 19 (NIV) Please fill in the blanks:

_____ you, O Lord, be not _____ _____; O my _____,

come quickly to help me.

Verse 20 (NIV) Please fill in the blanks:

_____ my life from the _____, my precious life from the _____

of the _____.

Verse 21(NIV) Fill in the blanks:

_____ me from the mouth of the _____; save me from the _____ of

the _____ _____.

You who fear the Lord, praise him! Revere him, all you descendants of Jacob, honor him! Revere him, all you descendants of Israel! (verse 23)

Verse 24 (NIV) Please fill in the blanks:

For he has not despised or disdained the _____ of the _____

_____; he has not hidden his face from him _____ has _____ to his

_____ _____ _____.

Verse 27 (NIV) Please fill in the blanks:

All the ends of the earth will remember and _____ to the Lord, and all the families of the nations will

bow down before him.

There is such good news that the God of Israel hears the prayers of his people and saves them. He moves them to turn from their wickedness as they learn to trust in him.

Verses 30-31 (NIV) Please fill in the blanks:

Posterity will _____ him; future generations will be told _____

_____ _____. They will proclaim his _____ to a people yet unborn—for he

_____ _____ _____.

Read John 19: 30 (NIV) Please fill in the blanks:

When he had received the drink, Jesus said, "_____ _____ _____." With

that, he bowed his head and gave up his spirit.

Philippians 2: 9-11

"Therefore God exalted him to the
highest place
and gave him the name that is
above every name,
that at the time of Jesus every knee
should bow,
in heaven and on earth and under
the earth,
and every tongue confess that Jesus
Christ is Lord,
to the glory of God the Father."

1.How different for you is the meaning of Psalm 22: 1, when it is taken in the context of the whole Psalm? Do you see it as a plea for help or a statement of fact? Do you believe that Jesus probably said the whole Psalm from the cross? What does this Psalm mean to you?

Abandoned and Forsaken — by Elaine

"My God, my God why have you forsaken me?" These are the words of Jesus spoken from the cross. When Craig died, I felt abandoned by God. If God could forsake his own son, why would he care about me?

Another stumbling block for me! How could God stand back and watch his own son tortured and then killed to resolve his issues with humans? Because he loves us? I didn't understand.

I didn't understand—that's a huge understatement. I had so little knowledge in the beginning of my journey through grief and even less wisdom. My faith was very superficial. I'd even call it a Santa Claus faith. Like a child, I would make my wants known to God and expect him to deliver. I believed scripture supported that. I was a good person, and David and I were in full-time ministry. We made sacrifices in order to work for God. Why wouldn't God shower me with every blessing?

My faith was largely based on my circumstances. When everything was going my way, I was ready to serve God faithfully. When tragedy came, like Job, I began to question God and his love for me.

I couldn't get the words that Jesus spoke from the cross out of my mind. Forsaken. He believed his Father had forsaken him. In the garden at Gethsemane, Jesus had pleaded with God in order that he wouldn't have to go to the cross. I had multiple questions.

When I learned that Jesus was reciting Psalm 22 in its entirety from the cross, my understanding changed. I realized that Jesus was making another plea to God. He was in effect saying, "Please help me. I *feel* forsaken. My forefathers trusted you and *were not disappointed.* The enemy is trying to destroy me. I'm so thirsty. I feel weakened. I need your strength. Come to me, Father. Draw near. It's finally over. Into your hands I commend my spirit." And now he lives, so that we can live. Therefore, Craig lives and never died.

Jesus came to show us God's love. He did that sacrificially. It has taken me years to understand that. I was desperate for God. I, too, was thirsty. He came to me. He supplied my need. I am grateful.

•••

Where Is Christ in This? — by David

Something happened, but what? The writer of Psalm 22 clearly had a change in his life somewhere between verses 21 and 22. This familiar Psalm quoted by the Christ while on the cross begins with words that I understand. I understand feelings of being forsaken by God. Yet, this Psalm ends with words of triumph and confidence.

"My God, my God why have you forsaken me?" How powerful and familiar are these words. I shouted such words often in those first years of grief. Where are you, God? The words echo a loneliness and despair that I know all too well. How well the first two verses describe my experience....

Eventually, I began to realize a profound truth. Where else could I turn? Psalm 22: 11 (NIV) tells me, "Do not be far from me, for trouble is near and there is no one to help."

OK, I thought to myself, I am committed to this path but where is it leading me? Where is God in all of this? Over the years I had learned to ask this question as a way to encounter God and Christ in my daily life, "Where is God in my life today?"

The psalmist continues with his cries for help until verse 22. Here, for whatever reason, he turns from despair to praise. The writer goes from "rescue me" to "I will praise you". Something happened, but what?

When I look back on the past years I know that I have moved from a time of complete devastation to a place of confidence in God that includes genuine praise. This has been a hard transition to make but it has been so necessary.

What happened to this writer that resulted in such a profound change in attitude toward God is unknown. We don't know the specifics of the conversion. We really don't know what experience Job had with God or what Paul's thorn in the flesh that he took to God, but we do know that they were profound and life-changing experiences. They encountered God and were never the same.

At some time in my life, hope began to emerge. I can't tell you the exact date or time or circumstance when this gift began to grow but two things I am confident about. One is that God has been with me throughout this horrible experience. I am aware that even at times when I didn't or couldn't acknowledge God's presence and His love for me, I knew he was with me. That makes all the difference in the world for me.

I am a child of God. I am part of a larger group of believers and seekers. I am also affirmed in my heart that I have great worth in God's eyes. This revelation makes a huge difference for me. I'm now confident of my value to God.

Somewhere in my recent past, I made a small movement from doubt and despair to belief. In a moment that I cannot recall, I began to move closer to God. I still get angry and depressed at times but those days are not as frequent.

Somewhere, somehow, and sometime, I moved from hurt and anger to confidence in God's love, not only for me but my family. I now trust God.

Week Eight
THE WORD BECAME FLESH

WEEK EIGHT
THE WORD BECAME FLESH

The fourth Gospel is believed by many scholars to be written by John, the beloved disciple of Jesus. John was probably just a boy when he walked with Jesus and witnessed all that he did. We believe he wrote the Gospel of John, the three Johns, and Revelation late in his life while he was in exile on the island of Patmos.

All of the other disciples had been martyred by this time including Paul. John was an old man, as it is believed that the date of his writings is between 90 and 100 A.D. John even witnessed the destruction of Jerusalem.

John's Gospel is much different than the other three. He didn't necessarily want to repeat what the other Gospels said about Jesus. He wanted to give his reader a few other accounts of what Jesus did for humanity. One of the central themes in his writings is that Jesus is the promised Messiah for whom the Jewish people had been waiting for. Jesus is the Word made flesh. God came in human form for one purpose—to show the world how much He loves us.

John mentions several times that he knows the things Jesus did because he witnessed them with his own eyes. He gives many details about Jewish life and the geography of the land that gives much credibility to his claims.

Above and beyond all else, John wants the world to know that God is love. In 1 John 4: 7-12, John writes:

> "Dear friends, let us love one another, for love comes from God. Everyone who loves has been born of God and knows God. Whoever does not love does not know God, because God is love. This is how God showed his love among us: He sent his one and only Son into the world that we might live through him. This is love: not that we loved God, but that he loved us and sent his Son as an atoning sacrifice for our sins. Dear friends, since God so loved us, we also ought to love one another. No one has ever seen God; but if we love one another, God lives in us and his love is made complete in us."

John, the eyewitness, knew that he was loved by Jesus and by his Father. John's name is not mentioned in his Gospel. He refers to himself as the disciple whom Jesus loved. He didn't speak out of arrogance but with great assurance deep within his heart that Jesus is the embodiment of God's love. He walked with Jesus and knew him intimately as a friend. He spent a lifetime meditating on his words and reflecting on his every move. He knows.

DAY 1: THE WORD

Open each day's study with this prayer or one of your own:

God, you are the same yesterday, today, and tomorrow.
Give us the courage to face this day with renewed strength and with hope.
Heal all our wounds and love us back to wholeness.

Amen

Read John 1: 1-51 (If time permits, it would be helpful to you if you read the entire Gospel of John).

Verses 1 & 2 (NIV) Please fill in the blanks:

In the beginning was the _____, and the _____ was _____

_____, and the _____ was _____. _____ was

_____ _____ in the beginning.

Notice that Word is capitalized indicating a proper noun. In verse two, we read that He was with God in the beginning. John is deliberately indicating that God came to earth in Jesus. The Greek for Word is logos, a term not only used for the spoken word but also of the unspoken word. It was the word of the mind or reason. In Jesus, the mind of God became a person. God's creative power, the mind that brought the world into existence and which gives light and life to everyone came through the Word, Jesus. Jesus became the word of God among us. The Word makes sense of the world. Jesus came not only to tell about God, but to show us the love that is God.

Genesis 1: 1 (NIV)

In the beginning, God created the heavens and the Earth.

John 1: 14 (NIV) Please fill in the blanks:

The _____ became flesh and made his dwelling among us. We have seen his _____,

the _____of the _____ and _____, who came from the

_____, full of _____ and _____.

Jesus revealed the glory of God. The life of Jesus was a manifestation of God's power and love. The splendor, which is the presence of God, was made visible in Jesus, and at the heart of that splendor was love. People began to see that God's glory and God's love were one and the same.

The One and Only (Jesus) came from the Father full of grace and truth. People had thought of God in terms of might and majesty, power and judgment. Many people thought God to be unapproachable, invisible, and unreachable. Jesus came to show us the undeserved and limitless kindness of God called grace. We see the loveliness of God in Jesus.

Jesus is the embodiment of the truth about God. To see Jesus is to see God. Jesus displayed the true character of God. He came to communicate the truth and to witness to the truth about God in such a way that he makes things clear. Many times in the NIV version of Jesus' words he says, "I tell you the truth." That truth is what we can stake our faith on.

Reread Verses 15-17 (NIV)

Verses 17 & 18 (NIV) Please fill in the blanks:

For the law was given through Moses; _____ and _____ came through

_____ _____. No one has ever seen God, but _____ the

_____ and _____, who is at the Father's side, has made him _____.

God the One and Only is an explicit declaration of Jesus' deity. Jesus was fully human and fully divine. It is through Jesus that God the law-giver has become God the Father. God the judge has become God the lover of human souls. Jesus alone can bring God to us and bring us to God.

1. How do you see God through Jesus? Is how you see God's character different from how you see Jesus' character?

In the beginning was the Word, the heart and mind of God. God hasn't changed. He is the same God that Moses, Abraham, and Jacob encountered. He is the same God that Job encountered. Jesus came to show us that God.

DAY 2: GOD SO LOVED THE WORLD

Opening Prayer:

God, you are the same yesterday, today, and tomorrow.
Give us the courage to face this day with renewed strength and with hope.
Heal all our wounds and love us back to wholeness.

Amen

Read John 3: 1-21

Nicodemus was a man of the Pharisees. The Pharisees were a group of men who governed the law of Moses. They devoted their entire life to keeping every minute point of law and making sure other Jews obeyed it as well. They had taken the law given to Moses and added many of their own interpretations. For instance, in keeping the Sabbath holy, a Jew could not carry a burden (load). Wearing sandals with nails in them was considered breaking the law. Nails constituted a burden. False teeth and artificial limbs were considered burdens. A Jewish person was not to work on the Sabbath. Healing was considered work. It became nearly impossible to keep the law. Jesus came not to abolish the law but to fulfill it. He came to show us God's intentions when he gave us the law. The law was not meant to govern what we do. Its intention is to govern our hearts.

Verse 3 (NIV) Please fill in the blanks:

In reply Jesus declared, "I tell you the _____, no one can see the kingdom of God unless he is

_____ _____."

Verse 5 (NIV)

Jesus answered, "I tell you the _____, no one can enter the kingdom of God unless he is

born of _____ and the _____."

Verse 11 (NIV) Please fill in the blank:

"I tell you the _____, we speak of what we know, and we testify to what we have seen, but still you people do not accept our testimony.

Jesus came to tell them and us the truth. The Pharisees had become so spiritually blinded that they couldn't recognize God. Their hearts had become hardened. All they could see was keeping the law. It didn't matter that they had become callous and uncaring. They believed a man who was righteous (right with God) obeyed the law. Jesus couldn't possibly be the Son of Man that was prophesied in Daniel (Daniel 7: 13-14) because he continually broke the law in favor of compassionate healing, loving, and caring for the needs of the people. By referring to himself as the Son of Man, Jesus is claiming that he is the promised Messiah or Savior.

Verse 16 (NIV) Please fill in the blanks:

"For _____ so _____ the world that he _____ his

one and only _____, that _____ believes in him shall not _____

but have _____ _____.

This is probably the first verse that we memorized as children. It has to be the most well-known verse of the Bible. It has become so common that perhaps we have missed its profound meaning. In the middle of Jesus words to the Pharisee, Nicodemus, we have this famous verse. Taken in context, Jesus is proclaiming to the religious leaders of that time that they have it all wrong. His message was one of supreme love from the Father. Jesus was proclaiming his position of authority as God's Son, his One and Only. He contradicted the idea that obedience to the law had the power to save.

Verse 17 (NIV) Please fill in the blanks:

For _____ did not _____ his _____ Into the world to

_____ the world, but to _____ the world _____ _____.

Verse 19 (NIV) Please fill in the blanks:

This is the verdict: _____ has come into the world, but men loved _____

instead of _____ because their deeds were evil.

A common theme in John's gospel is that Jesus came to bring light for the darkness. He is the Light of the world. In him there is no darkness (no evil).

1. What does it mean to you that Jesus is the Light of the world?

Jesus was without sin. He is our perfect example of how to live and pattern our life (Ephesians 4: 17-32) . Light is revealing. We see our mistakes and our sin as compared to him. We also see how freeing it is to live in the Light. A life lived hiding in darkness breeds selfish motives, hate, bitterness, and destruction. Relationships dissolve. Jesus came to show us how God desires us to live—in love and peace.

DAY 3: THE MIRACLES OF JESUS

Opening Prayer:

God, you are the same yesterday, today, and tomorrow.
Give us the courage to face this day with renewed strength and with hope.
Heal all our wounds and love us back to wholeness.

Amen

John uses signs for the miracles of God. The supreme thing about the miracles of Jesus was that they told people something about the character and nature of God. Miracles were not simply astonishing and powerful displays, they revealed to us something about how we can better understand God.

Read John 2: 1-11

Verse 9 (NIV) Please fill in the blanks:

and the master of the banquet tasted the _____ that had been turned into _____.

Verse 11 (NIV) Please fill in the blanks:

This, the first of his miraculous signs, Jesus performed at Cana in Galilee. He thus _____

his _____, and his disciples put their _____ in him.

Read John 4: 46-54

Verse 48 (NIV) Please fill in the blanks:

"Unless you people see _____ _____ and _____," Jesus

told him, "you will _____ _____.

Verse 50 (NIV) Please fill in the blanks:

Jesus replied, "You may go. Your _____ will _____.

Read John 5: 1-9

Verse 8 (NIV) Please fill in the blank:

Then Jesus said to him, "Get up! Pick up your mat and _____."

Read John 6: 6-13

Verses 9-11 (NIV) Please fill in the blanks:

Here is a boy with _____ _____ _____ _____and

_____ _____ _____, but how far will they go among so many?

Jesus said, "Have the people sit down," There was plenty of grass in that place, and the men sat down,

about _____ _____ of them. Jesus then took the loaves, gave thanks, and

_____ to those who were seated as _____ as they _____.

He did the same with the fish.

Read John 6: 16-21

Verse 19 (NIV) Please fill in the blanks:

When they had rowed three or three and a half miles, they saw _____ approaching the boat,

_____ on the _____; and they were terrified.

1. What do you understand about God through these miraculous signs performed by Jesus?

These miracles were either healing miracles or miracles showing God's power. They show God's loving desire to heal and provide for the needs of his people. They were astonishing and only something God could do. Many people became followers of Jesus because of the miracles he performed.

Read John 9: 1-12

Verses 1-3 (NIV) Please fill in the blanks:

As he went along, he saw a man blind from birth. His disciples asked him, "Rabbi, who sinned, this man or his parents, that he was born blind?" Neither this man nor his parents sinned," said Jesus, "but this happened so that the

_____ _____ _____ might be displayed in his life.

2. Does it trouble you that Jesus said that the man was born blind so that God's works might be displayed in his life?

Read John 9: 13-41

Verses 30-33 (NIV) Please fill in the blanks:

The man answered, "Now that is remarkable! You don't know where he comes from, yet he opened my

eyes. We know that _____ does not listen to _____. He listens to the godly

man who _____ his _____. Nobody has ever heard of opening the eyes of a

man born blind. If this man were _____ _____ _____, he could do

_____."

3. How did the blind man respond to his healing?

He responded in faith. He understood his healing as coming from God through a man without sin, Jesus.

4. What did Jesus do when he found out that the blind man had been thrown out by the Pharisees?

Jesus went looking for him. He revealed that he was the Messiah and the man believed and worshipped him. He healed his spiritual blindness, also.

John almost always has a deeper meaning in the stories he tells about Jesus. What he intends for his readers to see is how spiritually blind the Pharisees had become. They continuously tried to trap Jesus and missed God. Jesus' miracles were generating quite a stir. He was becoming very popular and many were following him and becoming his disciples. The Pharisees feared that their power and position were being threatened. Time and time again, Jesus boldly and blatantly contradicted their view of God. They became more and more angry at Jesus. So angry they plotted to kill him to shut him up.

DAY 4: "LAZARUS, COME OUT!"

Opening Prayer:

God, you are the same yesterday, today, and tomorrow.
Give us the courage to face this day with renewed strength and with hope.
Heal all our wounds and love us back to wholeness.

Amen

We have come to the reason we have titled this study guide, *"Lazarus, Come Out!"* The miracle of Lazarus' being raised from the dead took place shortly before Jesus' own death and resurrection.

Jesus had caused quite a stir among the religious leaders. The news of his miracles spread quickly. Many people were becoming disciples. The threat of civil disorder was concerning the Pharisees and the Sadducees.

The Sanhedrin was comprised of both Pharisees and Sadducees and was a group of about 70 men who had authority over the spiritual and temporal life of the Jewish people. It was assembled to deal with the situation.

The Pharisees were not a political party. Their sole concern was living according to every detail of the law. The Sadducees, however, were intensely political. They were the wealthy and aristocratic party. They were very committed to doing whatever was necessary to maintain their favorable relationship with the Roman government.

All the priests were Sadducees. They didn't believe in bodily resurrection. They were becoming intensely angry at what Jesus was doing. They didn't care if he was right or wrong. They judged things not in light of principle but whether their careers were protected. By this time, they were looking to kill Jesus. It was better that one man die (Jesus) than for them to risk death by the Romans.

Read John 11: 1-16

Verses 3-4 (NIV) Please fill in the blanks:

So the sisters sent word to Jesus, "Lord, the _____ _____ _____ is

sick." When he heard this, Jesus said, "This sickness will not end in death. No, it is for _____

_____ so that _____ _____ may be _____

through it.

Jesus' love for Mary, Martha, and Lazarus was always known to them and those around them. They were dear friends as well as disciples. Verse 6 tells us that when he heard that Lazarus was sick, he stayed for two more days.

It was dangerous for Jesus and his disciples to go back to Bethany. Bethany was only two miles from Jerusalem. He was well aware of the plot to kill him. It wasn't fear that made him linger.

He knew that Lazarus would be healed. Many would see God's glory in action including the Sadducees who didn't believe in the resurrection of the body. This healing would be his last attempt to open some blind eyes before he was glorified on the cross. He knew perfectly well that to go to Bethany and to cure Lazarus was to take a step which would end in the Cross—and it did. He showed them and us the Truth in God's Love.

Verse 14 (NIV) Please fill in the blanks:

So then he told them plainly, "Lazarus is dead, and _____ _____ _____

I am glad I was not there, so that you _____ _____. But let's go to him."

Read John 11: 17-37

Lazarus had been dead for four days. The belief at that time was that a person's spirit lingered for four days. After the fourth day, the person was considered dead in body and spirit. Many people were already there comforting the sisters of Lazarus, Mary and Martha.

Verse 21 (NIV) Please fill in the blanks:

"Lord," Martha said to Jesus, "if you _____ _____ _____, my brother

would _____ _____ _____. But I know that even now God will give you

whatever you ask."

1. Who has the power to heal?

God heals through Jesus.

Verse 23 (NIV) Please fill in the blanks:

Jesus said to her, "Your brother will _____ _____."

Verse 24 (NIV) Fill in the blanks:

Martha answered, "I know he will rise again in the _____ _____ _____

_____ _____."

In Old Testament times, people had practically no belief in life after death. It was believed that people went to Sheol, and there they lived a vague, shadowy, weak, joyless, ghostly kind of life. In the days of Jesus, the Sadducees still refused to believe in any life after death. All priests were Sadducees. But the Pharisees and the great majority of the Jews did believe in life after death. When Martha answered Jesus as she did, she bore witness to her belief that there is life after death.

Verse 25-26 (NIV) Please fill in the blanks:

Jesus said to her, "I am the _____ and the _____. He who

_____ in me will _____, even though he _____;

and whoever _____ and _____ in me will _____

_____. Do you believe this? "Yes, Lord," she told him, "I believe that you are the _____,

the _____ of _____, who was to come into the world.

Verse 35 (NIV) Please fill in the blank:

Jesus _____.

2. This is the shortest verse in the Bible. Jesus wept certainly because he loved Lazarus. However, he also knew that he was going to raise him from the dead. Even though the scriptures don't tell us, what other reasons might have caused Jesus to weep?

Read John 11: 38-44

Verse 40 (NIV) Please fill in the blanks:

Then Jesus said, "Did I not tell you that if you _____, you would see the

_____ of _____?"

Verses 41-42 (NIV) Please fill in the blanks:

So they took away the stone. Then Jesus looked up and said, "_____, I thank you that you

have heard me. I _____ that you _____ hear me, but I said this for

the _____ of the people standing here, that they may _____ that you

_____ me."

What Jesus wanted people to know the most was that he was sent by God as the Christ (Messiah) to show them and us the glory of God that is Love.

Verse 43 (NIV) Please fill in the blanks:

When he had said this, Jesus called out in a loud voice, "Lazarus, _____ _____!"

Verse 44 (NIV) Please fill in the blanks:

The _____ man came out, his hands and feet wrapped with strips of linen, and a cloth around

his face. Jesus said to them, "Take off the _____ _____ and _____

_____ _____.

Enough said! The resurrection is for all believers.

DAY 5: JESUS WASHES HIS DISCIPLES' FEET

Opening Prayer:

God, you are the same yesterday, today, and tomorrow.
Give us the courage to face this day with renewed strength and with hope.
Heal all our wounds and love us back to wholeness.

Amen

After Jesus raised Lazarus from the dead he knew his life was in danger. He withdrew to a region near the desert, to a village called Ephraim, where he stayed with his disciples (John 11: 45-54). Not out of fear, but in careful timing did Jesus withdraw from the crowds.

Six days before the Passover Jesus arrived at Bethany, two miles from Jerusalem. He stayed at the home of Lazarus, Martha, and Mary and from there made his triumphant entry into Jerusalem (John 12: 1-50)

Read John 13: 1-17

Verses 3-5 (NIV) Please fill in the blanks:

Jesus knew that the _____ had put all things under his _____, and

that he _____ _____ _____ _____ and was

_____ to God; so he got up from the meal, took off his outer clothing, and wrapped a towel

around his waist. After that, he poured water into a basin and began to _____ _____

_____ _____, drying them with the towel that was wrapped around him.

It was the evening meal. Jesus and his disciples were in the upper room sharing a last meal together. This meal normally would have been a time of celebration, commemorating God's setting the Israelites free from the bondage of the Egyptians. This was Jesus' last opportunity to teach his disciples. It was a solemn occasion. The disciples were confused at his teaching. They weren't argumentative, they simply didn't understand.

Verses 6-7 (NIV) Please fill in the blanks:

He came to Simon Peter, who said to him, "Lord, are you going to wash my feet? Jesus replied, "You do not realize now what I am doing, but _____ you will _____."

1. What was Peter's reaction to Jesus wanting to wash his feet?

Maybe it was embarrassment, pride, or humility, but Peter didn't want Jesus to wash his feet.

2. How did Jesus respond to Peter? (verses 10-17)

Jesus didn't rebuke Peter. He lovingly understood him. Peter had been with Jesus for three years at this point. Jesus was turning the common Jewish beliefs upside down. He knew his disciples wouldn't understand then, but they would when they looked back after the resurrection and ascension.

Essentially what Jesus wanted Peter to understand then was that unless Jesus washed his feet, he couldn't be a part of the Church later. All of his disciples needed to see the example of Christian love set by Jesus.

Read John 13: 18-30

3. What did Jesus already know about Judas? (verses 18-30)

Jesus knew that Judas was going to betray him. The disciples and Jesus were reclining at the table. They would have been reclining on low couches with their left elbow on the table leaving their right hand open with which to eat. The table would have three parts shaped in a u. Jesus would have been in the center. The disciple whom Jesus loved (none other than John himself) was on his right leaning into Jesus' breast. Because we know that Judas was close enough to Jesus that Jesus had an intimate conversation with him and that he was able to give him a piece of bread, we can assume that Judas was on his left. This place was considered the place of honor at the table and was reserved for a person who the host considered a loyal and trusted friend. Jesus was making one final attempt to reach Judas' heart.

Read John 13: 31-38

Jesus knew the time was near. Only Jesus knew exactly what was going to happen. He is telling his disciples that he is going to a place where they couldn't come. He was leaving them with one new commandment.

Verses 34-35 (NIV) Please fill in the blanks:

"A new command I give you: _____ _____ _____.

As I have _____ you so you must _____ _____

_____. By this all men will know that you are my _____, if you

_____ _____ _____.

4. *What did Jesus already know about Peter?*

Before the cock crows, Peter would deny him three times. He also knew that the other disciples would abandon him. Yet, he washed their feet.

5. How does Jesus love his disciples? What was the example that Jesus wants his disciples to follow?

In the face of cruel betrayal, denial, and abandonment, Jesus washed his disciples' feet. The example Jesus set was one of *selfless* love. Jesus knew the end from the beginning. Jesus never thought of himself. He gave all he had for those he loved.

He loved them *sacrificially.* If love meant the Cross, he was prepared to go there. Love cost him his life. No greater love has a man than to lay down his life for his friends. Jesus knew that the only way to save the world was through love. How else would the world know the Way to victory?

He loved his disciples knowing their human weaknesses. He knew they would fail. He also knew that forgiveness would be given to them. Jesus held nothing against them. He *showed* them nothing but love and broke their hearts which is the way to repentance and forgiveness. That's the power in God's love, grace, and mercy shown to the world by Jesus through the Cross. The disciples closest to Jesus saw numerous miracles. They saw the powerful might of God. It was through Love that they saw their sinfulness and need for repentance. Perfect Love ushered in a whole new way of Life. It empowers the world to live with passion and in peace and joy.

My Father's Daughter — by Elaine

For far too much of my life, Jesus and God had very different personalities in my mind. Jesus was kind, compassionate, gentle, and loving. God was the polar opposite. He was stern, strict, unapproachable, and if I wasn't careful I would suffer his wrath.

Therefore, I didn't trust God because I didn't think he even liked me much less loved me. I spent most of the time trying to hide from God, especially hiding how I really felt about him. I thought God was easily angered so I avoided any contact with him. My prayers to Jesus were heartfelt. My prayers to God were desperate pleas for mercy. I never felt as if I measured up or would ever be good enough to please God.

It wasn't until I started studying the writings of John who called himself the beloved disciple that I began to see the truth about God. It's so clear to me now that I feel ashamed for my ignorance. I had all of these preconceived notions about God that weren't supported in scripture. I had no idea they weren't supported in scripture because I hadn't read it. It's amazing what I learned when I actually started studying the Bible. God changed!

Of course God didn't change, I changed my mind about God. John's gospel has as a central theme: If you've seen Jesus, you've seen God. They are One. God was the same from before the foundation of the world. He didn't change after Jesus came. Jesus came to show us the true character of God.

There was a huge transformation in me when I actually saw God in Jesus and Jesus in God. I started to trust God. I now know He loves me and sometimes He even delights in me. I have become my Father's daughter and joint heir with his Son, Jesus to kingdom life. I pray often to my Abba, Father. I understand his love as the same unconditional love that I have for my children and grandchildren. There is nothing that they can do to make me stop loving them. Love never fails. God will never leave nor forsake me.

I'm awestruck. One of the most amazing discoveries I have found about God is seeing his love for Job. Job's encounter with God was transforming. Job said he saw the face of God. He saw God's love as well as his sovereignty. What Job encountered was a God that was like Jesus. They are One.

Every encounter with God is like encountering Jesus. That realization monumentally changed my heart to accept God's love. I always felt Jesus loved me. Now I know God's love also, and I'm better able to trust God with Craig.

•••

No Longer an Outsider — by David

John's Gospel has become so important to my journey. This non-synoptic gospel at first seemed so strange. It had to grow on me, and it has. Its overarching message has carried me through some tough years. John wants us to know that God and Jesus are one and the same. John stresses that Jesus is the revelation and presence of God. "When you have seen me and when you hear me," Jesus says again and again, "You have seen and heard God."

For longer than I care to admit, God seemed harsh and scary. I, like so many people, viewed God as the angry, vengeful, and sovereign God crushing opposing armies and destroying people who have sinned. The God of the Old Testament is sometimes hard to like, much less love. This was another issue to deal with in the reconstruction of my faith.

My thinking had to grow and stretch through the work of the Holy Spirit. I, at first, thought that the Old Testament God is different than the New Testament God. I rejected this line of thought after a period of time. God is the same yesterday, today, and tomorrow. God's character is eternal. Therefore, there had to be another way of understanding.

Then I started to seriously read and study the Gospel of John. God and Jesus are one and the same. Admittedly, a difficult concept for our finite minds to fully understand, but it's an essential truth within the Christian faith. So, I began to wonder what this Gospel has to say about the character of God.

I mulled over that concept for quite some time. God and Jesus are one.

What did that mean to me now that my Craig was not physically present any more? I don't recall exactly when I began this thread of thought or when I came to a place of comfort by taking it to heart.

Some scholars talk about incarnational theology. By this they mean a way of understanding God and Christ through Jesus' taking on human form and living with other human beings. This is a uniquely Christian claim. It wasn't until the whole meaning of the word "Logos," as John talks about it in chapter 1, started to settle in my mind that I began to let go of my anger toward God. It was when I realized that Jesus had modeled the true character of God, that this wide breach between God and me began to close.

John's Gospel opens with, "The Word became flesh and lived among us."

Jesus is the eternal Word, and as John also tells us, this Word of God was God.

A theology of the incarnation teaches that God made what was abstract and difficult to understand concrete and accessible. It teaches that God has revealed God's self through normal events and a human person.

I have learned in the rebuilding of my faith after Craig's death, that persistent inquiry is eventually honored. Here are some verses from John that have brought hope back to my life.

I speak only of what I know by experience; I give witness only to what I have seen with my own eyes. There is nothing secondhand here, no hearsay.

John 3:11 (Message)

Jesus said, "Everyone who drinks this water will get thirsty again and again. Anyone who drinks the water I give will never thirst—not ever. The water I give will be an artesian spring within, gushing fountains of endless life."

John 4: 13-14 (Message)

So Jesus explained himself at length, "I'm telling you this straight. The Son can't independently do a thing, only what he sees the Father doing. What the Father does, the Son does. The Father loves the Son and includes him in everything he is doing.

John 5: 19-20 (Message)

It's urgent that you listen carefully to this: Anyone here who believes what I am saying right now and aligns himself with the Father, who has in fact put me in charge, has at this very moment the real, lasting life and is no longer condemned to be an outsider. This person has taken a giant step from the world of the dead to the world of the living.

John 5: 24 (Message)

I can't do a solitary thing on my own: I listen, then I decide. You can trust my decision because I'm not out to get my own way but only to carry out orders. If I were simply speaking on my own account, it would be an empty, self-serving witness. But an independent witness confirms me, the most reliable Witness of all. Furthermore, you all saw and heard John, and he gave expert and reliable testimony about me, didn't he?

John 5: 30-33 (Message)

God loves me and cares for me as much as Jesus. I am still learning what this insight really means but I know that it is important and has opened up to me the possibility of hope.

❦

Week Nine

THE WAY, TRUTH, AND LIFE

WEEK NINE
THE WAY, TRUTH, AND LIFE

In a very short time the disciples' lives would be radically changed forever. Jesus wanted them to know what was about to happen and how he would be with them every step of the way. In fact, John takes four chapters telling the reader the words Jesus spoke in the upper room.

Jesus truly loved them and wanted to prepare them so that when the horrific events took place in the near future they would know that God was with him. Jesus knew they wouldn't understand until he completed what he had come to do from the beginning.

Jesus knew the persecution they would face for following him. He cared deeply that they were about to suffer as they took up their own cross to share the message of hope and love with the world. He wasn't giving them an easy task. He knew that the same Father who walked with him giving him the strength to endure would be with them.

Jesus came to show the world the Way, the Truth, and the Life. He was and is our example from which we need to pattern our life. The way to abundant life is through love—pure and simple yet difficult at times. There will be times when that kind of love costs us something. It's easy to love the loveable and so hard to love our enemies. That's precisely what Jesus commands of his followers. Jesus tells all of us, "If you love me, you'll obey me (John 14: 21). This is my command: Love each other (John 15: 17)."

The Way to the Father is through sacrificial love. Chapter 17 records a love-filled prayer by Jesus. First he prays for himself, "And now, Father, glorify me in your presence with the glory I had with you before the world began." Jesus understood that the reward is great.

He then prayed for his disciples, "I will remain in the world no longer, but they are still in the world, and I am coming to you, Holy Father, protect them by the power of your name—the name you gave me—so they may be one as we are one." The reward is great for following Jesus.

Jesus then prayed for all believers saying, "My prayer is not for them alone, I pray also for those who will believe in me through their message, that all of them may be one, Father, just as you are in me and I am in you." He continues, "May they be brought to complete unity to let the world know that you sent me and have loved them even as you have loved me." Jesus is the Way, the Truth, and the Life. As God is love, He is love. All he asks from the Cross is that we love each other.

DAY 1: JESUS COMFORTS HIS DISCIPLES

Open each day's study with this prayer or one of your own:

Merciful God, help us this day and every day to love others as you have loved us. Thank you for that love and our supreme example to follow in your Son, Jesus. May that love shine through me.

Amen

Read John 14: 1-4

Verse 1(NIV) Please fill in the blanks:

"Do not let your hearts be troubled. _____ in God; _____ also in me.

1. What is Jesus going to do?

He tells his disciples that his Father's house has many rooms and that he is going to prepare a place for them. He is coming back for them so that where he is they will be also.

Read John 14: 5-13

Verse 6 (NIV) Please fill in the blanks:

Jesus answered, "I am the _____ and the _____ and the _____.
No one comes to the Father except through me.

2. What do you think Jesus meant by what he said?

This would have had great meaning for a Jew. Jesus claimed to be *the* Way. To walk in the way meant to follow God's commands and laws. Jesus, in effect, said to walk exactly like he walked to know the ways of God. They needed to follow his lead and guiding.

Jesus is *the* Truth. He is the living embodiment of the truth about God's love and character. He exemplifies moral truth. He lived the truth.

Jesus said that he was *the* Life. Jesus leads us to a life worth living. He lights our path. In him there is no darkness at all. He is the way to peace and joy.

No one comes to the Father except through him. He alone is the way to God. In him alone we see what God is like and how we find our way to the presence of God.

Verse 9 (NIV) Please fill in the blanks:

Jesus answered: "Don't you know me, Philip, even after I have been among you such a long time? Anyone who

has _____ _____ has _____ the _____. How can

you say, 'Show us the Father'?

Read John 14: 15-30

Verse 16 (NIV) Please fill in the blanks:

And I will ask the Father, and he will give you another _____ to be with you forever—the

_____ of _____.

Jesus tells his disciples that he won't leave them as orphans. He is sending them the Spirit of Truth. The image he gives is that he won't leave them without parental guidance.

Verse 23 (NIV) Please fill in the blanks:

Jesus replied, "If anyone loves me, he will _____ my _____.

My _____ will _____ him, and _____ will come to him and

_____ _____ _____ with him."

Verses 25-26 (NIV) Please fill in the blanks:

"All this I have spoken while still with you. But the _____, the _____

_____, whom the _____ will send in _____ _____, will

_____ you all things and will _____ you of everything I have said to you.

3. What will the Holy Spirit do?

We want to emphasize that the Holy Spirit will teach us the truth about God when we read his Word (the Bible). He will also remind us of all the that Jesus taught in the Word. The Holy Spirit makes the Bible the Living Word. He makes the Bible relevant for today.

Verse 27 (NIV) Please fill in the blanks:

"_____ I leave with you; my _____ I give you. I do not give to you as the

world gives. Do not let your hearts be troubled and do not be afraid."

4. What is meant by "What the world gives"?

John refers to the world as people who don't believe in God. They are controlled by the powers of darkness or Satan. That peace means free from war. The peace Jesus offers is peace of mind and heart.

DAY 2: I AM THE VINE

Opening Prayer:

Merciful God, help us this day and every day to love others as you have loved us. Thank you for that love and our supreme example to follow in your Son, Jesus. May that love shine through me.

Amen

Read John 15: 1-17

The vine is a common Old Testament symbol for Israel. Jesus tells his disciples "I am" the true vine. He is working with the religious heritage of the Jews. Basically, what he is saying is that the Jews think that because they belong to the branch of Israel, they are the true vine of God. Jesus tells them that he is the vine of God and that the branches must be joined to him.

Verses 9-11 (NIV) Please fill in the blanks:

"As the Father has loved me, so have I loved you. Now _____ in my love. If you

_____ my commands, you will _____ in my love, just as I have _____

my Father's commands and _____ in his love. I have told you this so that _____

_____ may be _____ you and that your _____ may be complete.

Jesus' disciples are chosen for joy. His disciple is a sinner redeemed because of Jesus. Therein lies complete joy. Jesus shows his disciples how to live in such a way that they remain in the love or presence of God.

Verses 13-15 (NIV) Please fill in the blanks:

"Greater love has no one than this, that he lay down his _____ for his _____. You are my

_____ if you do what I command. I no longer call you _____, because a servant does

not know his master's business. Instead, I have called you _____, for everything that I learned

from my Father I have made known to you."

Read John 15: 18-27

Verse 18 (NIV) Please fill in the blanks:

"If the world _____ _____, keep in mind that it _____

_____ first."

Jesus is telling his disciples that they will be persecuted as he is persecuted. Those who hate Jesus hate the One who sent him—God. He also tells them before he goes that the Spirit of Truth will testify about him.

Verse 27 (NIV) Please fill in the blanks:

"And you also must _____, for you have been with me from the beginning.

1. What would you testify as the Truth at this point in your journey?

DAY 3: THE SPIRIT OF TRUTH

Opening Prayer:

Merciful God, help us this day and every day to love others as you have loved us. Thank you for that love and our supreme example to follow in your Son, Jesus. May that love shine through me.

Amen

Read John 16: 1-4

Jesus again tells his disciples that they will be persecuted and even thrown out of the synagogue. This time he even mentions that they will be killed for their devotion to him.

Read John 16: 5-16

Verses 6-7 (NIV) Please fill in the blanks:

"Because I have said these things, you are filled with _____. But I _____

_____ _____ _____; It is for your _____ that I am going away. Unless

I go away, the _____ will not come to you; but if I go, _____ will send him to you.

1. Why is Jesus sending the Counselor?

The Counselor will come to convict the world of guilt in regard to sin and righteousness and judgment. The prince of this world now stands condemned. The Counselor will also testify to the Truth.

Verse 13 (NIV) Please fill in the blanks:

But when he, the _____ of _____, comes, he will _____ you

into all _____.

Read John 16: 17-33

Verse 20 (NIV) Please fill in the blanks:

"I tell you the truth, you will _____ and _____ while the world

_____. You will _____, but your _____ will turn to

_____."

Because Jesus is going to the Father, the disciples will grieve for a while. They will think that he is lost for good. At this point, they don't realize that Jesus will be resurrected. Jesus knows they don't understand. However, by telling them what is about to happen, they will understand when it actually happens. It's important that he explains the details from his own mouth while still with them.

Verses 30-33 (NIV) Please fill in the blanks:

Now we can see that you know all things and that you do not even need to have anyone ask you questions. This

makes us believe that you _____ from _____.

"You believe at last! Jesus answered. But a time is coming and has come, when you will be scattered,

each to his own home. You will leave me all _____. Yet I am not _____, for

my _____ is _____ _____. I have told you these things,

so that in me you may have _____. In _____ _____ you

will have _____. But take heart! I have _____ _____

_____."

The disciples have no idea what is about to happen. Fear will overtake them. They won't understand why Jesus will choose to die when he has the power to call 10,000 angels to his aide. He's determined to show the world the power in God's love. He will overcome the world. Evil will not hold him to the Cross.

2. What truth have you heard from the Holy Spirit (the Counselor) in today's study?

3. What does it mean to you that you are a friend of God?

DAY 4: JESUS PRAYS

Opening Prayer:

Merciful God, help us this day and every day to love others as you have loved us. Thank you for that love and our supreme example to follow in your Son, Jesus. May that love shine through me.

Amen

Chapter 17 of John contains three prayers that Jesus prays in the upper room only hours before his arrest. Jesus continuously understands the need for his Father to be near for strength and guidance. Jesus also knows how much his disciples will need to draw on the Father's strength in the short time to come.

Read John 17: 1-5

1. For whom and for what does Jesus pray?

Jesus prays for himself. The Cross that he was about to endure was the climax of his earthly ministry. He understood that the connection between the Cross and the world was to bring God's glory. God's glory would be represented in eternal life for the believer. It was time for Jesus to stay focused on the prize. Jesus' glory would come when he had accomplished the task he was sent to do. He was obedient to the will of God and God's desire to *show* his deep love for the Son and all of the world. Jesus' life wasn't taken. He gave his life freely to defeat the powers of evil and death through sin.

Read John 17: 6-19

2. For whom and for what does Jesus pray?

Jesus prays for his disciples. Jesus prays, "Holy Father, protect them by the power of your name—the name you gave me—so that they may be one as we are one."

Jesus prays that his disciples will be protected from the same hatred that will nail him to the Cross. He doesn't ask that they will be taken from it but that they will be able to face it by his example. They will be able to defeat the forces of evil with God's love and mercy. Then the world will truly know that they are his disciples.

Jesus prays that his disciples will know the full measure of *his joy* within them. His entire time with them was designed for the time when they would be filled to the full measure with God's love and the joy of his presence within them.

Ephesians 3: 18-19 (Amplified)

That you may have the power and be strong to apprehend and grasp with all the saints [God's devoted people, the experience of that love] what is the breadth and length and height and depth [of it].

[That you may really come] to know [practically, through experience for yourselves] the love of Christ, which far surpasses mere knowledge [without experience]; that you may be filled [through all your being] unto all the fullness of God [may have the richest measure of the divine Presence, and become a body wholly filled and flooded with God Himself]!

Read John 17: 20-26

3. For whom and for what does Jesus pray?

Jesus prays for all believers. Jesus prays, "My prayer is not for them alone. I pray also for those who will believe in me through their message."

Jesus prays that all believers will *know* the love of God from within. He prays that all believers will be in complete unity to the message that Jesus was sent by God to *show* the world God's love. Jesus prayed that the world would know that the love that was in him (Jesus) was not only available to the believer, but that it was his desire for *all* the world to know it.

Verse 25 (NIV) Please fill in the blanks:

"_____ Father, though the world does not _____ you, I _____ you, and they know that you have sent me. I have made you _____ to them, and will continue to make you _____ in order that the _____ you have for me may be

_____ them and that _____ myself may be _____ them."

4. Express your thoughts to God either in writing or in silent prayer.

DAY 5: JESUS IS ARRESTED

Opening Prayer:

Merciful God, help us this day and every day to love others as you have loved us. Thank you for that love and our supreme example to follow in your Son, Jesus. May that love shine through me.

Amen

John spends five chapters detailing the events in the upper room. He moves from there very quickly to Jesus' arrest. He spends very little time in the Garden of Gethsemane. Therefore, we will digress from John for a little while.

Read Matthew 26: 36-45

Jesus is no longer praying in the upper room. He and his disciples have gone into the night and passed through the Kidron Valley. On the other side was an olive grove. In this olive grove was the Garden of Gethsemane. Jesus told his disciples to wait at the entrance and he went a little farther to *pray*.

He took Peter, James, and John a little farther with him and said:

Verse 38 (NIV) Please fill in the blanks:

"My _____ is overwhelmed with _____ to the point of _____. Stay here and keep watch with me."

Jesus was distraught to the point of death. He knew he was about to face Satan head on. He would need strength beyond his own to overcome.

Verse 40 (NIV) Please fill in the blanks:

Then he returned to his disciples and found them _____. "Could you men not keep

watch with me for one hour?" He asked Peter, "Watch and _____ so that you will not fall into

_____. The _____ is willing but the _____ is weak.

Pray with me that you don't fall into temptation. Jesus was fighting his own battle with temptation—to the point that Luke records that blood fell like big drops. His human anguish was almost more than he could bear. Couldn't his closest friends stay awake one hour and help him pray.

Read Luke 22: 39-46

Verses 42-43 (NIV) Please fill in the blanks:

"Father, if you are willing, take this cup from me; yet not my will, but yours be done." An _____

from heaven appeared to him and _____ him.

Mark 14: 36 (NIV)

"Abba, Father," he said, "everything is possible for you. Take this cup from me.

Yet not what I will, but what you will."

Jesus prayed to his Abba, Father—his daddy. Jesus was in constant prayer to God. He knew he wasn't alone. He knew he was weak without him but he faced all that was about to happen with courage. God would provide strength every step of the way. God walked *with* him.

1. Take some time to pray as a child of God to your Abba, Father.

Read John 18: 1-11
Read Matthew 26: 47-56

Verses 49-50 (NIV) Please fill in the blanks:

Going at once to Jesus, Judas said, "Greetings, Rabbi!" and _____ _____. Jesus

replied, "_____, do what you came for."

Judas, the disciple, betrays Jesus with a kiss. Yet Jesus calls him friend. Judas had no idea what was about to happen to Jesus. He had seen the mighty power of God displayed many times in many miracles. Who would have thought that Jesus was prepared to die for even Judas? Jesus never retreated in fear. He *showed* nothing but love to the bitter end.

Jesus was arrested. Peter drew his sword and cut off the ear of a servant of the high priest.

Verse 52 (NIV) Please fill in the blanks:

"Put your sword back in its place," Jesus said to him, "for all who _____ the _____ will _____ by the sword. Do you think I cannot call on my _____, and he will at once put at my disposal more than _____ _____ of _____?

Jesus was about to show the world a new way to the Father. Jesus picked up the ear of the high priest's servant and placed it back where it belonged—he healed him. One more miracle that went unnoticed because of hate. In the face of betrayal, denial, abandonment, and shear hatred Jesus didn't retaliate. Love was about to conquer all. One new commandment Jesus left his disciples. Love one another as I have loved you.

Matthew 27: 3-4 (NIV)

When Judas, who had betrayed him, saw that Jesus was condemned, he was seized with remorse and returned the thirty silver coins to the chief priests and the elders. "I have sinned," he said, "for I have betrayed innocent blood."

2. Would Judas have recognized his sin had Jesus not shown him love to the bitter end?

Love changes people whom violence, revenge, and hate could never reach. Jesus washed Judas' feet. He seated him at a place of honor at the Last Supper meal together. He let him know repeatedly that he was aware of what Judas was about to do. Judas betrayed him with a kiss. Jesus called him his friend. When it was all said and done, he asked the Father to forgive him for Judas did not understand the need to pray against temptation. Satan is very crafty. He appealed to Judas' worldly nature. Jesus loved Judas. It was that love that changed Judas' heart. He was so full of guilt and shame at the recognition of his sinfulness that he hung himself. Had Judas waited three days to see Jesus prevail victoriously over that guilt and shame, he could have been forgiven.

My Abba, Father — by Elaine

I have watched Joyce Meyer for years. She is a nationally and internationally known teacher and preacher of God's Word. She lives in Fenton, Missouri and has a television program that is titled *Enjoying Everyday Life*.

Her story began when she was a very young child. Her father sexually abused her for most of her young life. Her mother knew what was happening but didn't do anything to stop it. She married young and in that marriage she suffered more abuse, mostly emotional. That marriage ended in divorce.

She married her current husband, Dave, and has been married many years. She openly gives her audience the details of her way back to God. She felt a call on her life to teach the Word as a young woman. She tells of teaching the Word to about 25 women sitting on her living room floor in short shorts and blowing cigarette smoke in their faces. She has matured in her faith before millions of people. I believe that is her appeal, especially to women. She is so real in her struggle to live her life in faith with so much *reason* in her past not to have any relationship with God much less a loving one.

She desired God so much that she eventually was able to forgive her father and all the rest of the many hurtful people in her past. She could have become a bitter old woman and no one could blame her. God's love allowed her to find her value and self worth in him. She was able with God's help to confront her father. He asked her for forgiveness and the mean-spirited, gruff, and cruel alcoholic was changed by God's grace and mercy. Love changed his life. Joyce baptized him and he lived a short time thereafter. He died in peace with God.

Love changes things. The more I am enabled by the Holy Spirit to respond in love to the hurtful people in my life, the more peace and joy I have in my life. I have learned to find my value and self-worth in who I am in Christ. I'm better able to pray for my enemies. I'm better able to let go of the past pain in my life. I'm more at peace with losing Craig. I'm better able to allow my heart to let Craig rest in the Presence of God.

I'm a child of God. The example of God's love shown to me through the walk Jesus walked to and through the Cross has enlightened my way back to God, the Father. When I question his love, I look to the Cross.

•••

Where Was God? — by David

After the Compassionate Friends National Conference in Portland, Oregon that Elaine and I attended, we went to a Pacific seacoast town for a few days of relaxation. Since it was my first opportunity to actually see the Pacific we didn't waste much time getting from the resort to the beach. It was wonderful.

After a few minutes of watching families and people playing in the surf or simply enjoying the beach itself, we walked down to beach ourselves. To our right was the ocean and to our left were the hotels, resorts, and businesses of the town with the mountains behind them. It is then that I came upon a sign like I had never seen before. It read:

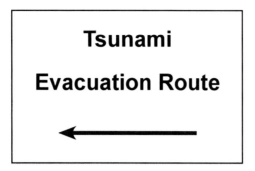

The arrow on the sign pointed away from the ocean and beach to the mountains on the opposite side of town.

I started to chuckle. It occurred to me that if a twenty foot wall of water were to suddenly appear out on the horizon moving toward the beach, I wouldn't have too much difficulty figuring out which way I would need to run. The sign seemed to me to be obvious.

It would be so helpful if all the signs in our lives were as obvious. Sometimes they are. However, there are circumstances so dark and so difficult that the signs laid out before us in our journey are indistinguishable. Craig's accident was such a time in my life.

Desperately clinging to any shred of hope has brought about some unexpected insights. I wondered, in those first months, did God really care about my struggles. If God did care, then why was there no intervention? Was God uncaring? Was God impotent to do anything? Was there some other way of understanding? Was I being blasphemous by pursuing such thoughts?

When the bits of clarity began to open up, I was amazed at the depth of God's love and also the deep significance of issues of faith that I thought I had grasped. In an earlier week, I shared thoughts about God and Jesus being one and the same and what that now means to my faith. I share another thought that now seems so obvious and yet wasn't obvious until recently.

The verses of scripture we have lifted up this week, for me, have one common thread—they all deal in their own way with the reality of evil in our world. They speak about the human condition and the response of our God to such sinfulness.

I have had some up close encounters with evil. Much of my employment before entering into public ministry was in the area of corrections. I have met men and women whose evil was palpable. Shortly after Craig's accident our country had the terrorism attacks of 9-11. Instantly, we had thousands of dead and dying people on our television sets, and in some way or another all Americans have had to reconstruct their view of life and their world. Our world suddenly became a more fearful place. Our world was not as predictable. Suddenly the "why" questions were on everyone's mind.

There was at least one question following 9-11 that bereaved parents also asked—Where was God? That question haunted my spiritual recovery as well. It still does at times. This Bible study is not an exercise in theodicy, which is a fancy theological term that describes attempts to explain evil and suffering, but we have nibbled around the edges of these very real issues.

And yet, certain things have been revealed in response to honest inquiry. I am more confident that God is present when evil occurs. I now believe that God was there when the car in which my son was a passenger swerved to avoid a white truck that failed to obey a stop sign. I understand now that God's heart is broken as well as mine at such times in my life.

I know that God has gone to elaborate lengths to lead his people away from those things and forces that would separate them from their Creator. Now this may well be basic Christianity 101 for many people, but for me these truths in the scriptures had to be rediscovered through the lens of profound grief.

I could go on, but my journey is not your journey. I hope that you have gained in your appreciation for God's passionate desire to not simply eliminate but destroy all the evil forces that work to separate you and me from our Creator.

Week Ten

TEARS IN A BOTTLE

WEEK TEN
TEARS IN A BOTTLE

Many people fear the end times. The *Revelation* is most likely the reason. It's strange to say the least and many people shy away from reading it. It's difficult to grasp the meaning behind the symbolism. Many religious eccentrics have portrayed very misleading ideas about this symbolism.

Not all scholars agree that John the disciple wrote *Revelation*. We accept the traditional view that the author was in fact the disciple of Jesus. If this is true, we have to remember that John was relentless in his pursuit of the Truth in Jesus the Christ. John, the beloved disciple, received the *Revelation* while in exile on Patmos. He used symbolism so that only the disciples would understand and yet not be in danger of persecution. The Roman authorities at this time were beginning to enforce emperor worship. Christians were being forced to declare that Caesar and not Jesus was Lord or face persecution. Outside of Jesus' disciples, it was a strange story of nonsense.

Remember the themes of John's Gospel when reading *Revelation*. Jesus **always** pointed to the love that is God, the Father. The *Revelation* is meant to be read as a source of comfort for the faithful believer.

John also writes to encourage the believer to remain faithful in resisting emperor worship. The final showdown between God and Satan is imminent. The faithful will be sealed against spiritual harm and will be vindicated when Jesus returns for his own disciples and the wicked will be destroyed forever. God's children will be with him into eternity.

"Therefore, they are before the throne of God and serve him day and night in his temple;
and he who sits on the throne will spread his tent over them.
Never again will they hunger; never again will they thirst. The sun will not beat upon them
nor any scorching heat.
For the Lamb at the center of the throne will be their shepherd; he will lead them to springs of
living water; And God will wipe away every tear from their eyes."
Revelation 7: 15-17 (NIV)

DAY 1: WHAT IS TRUTH?

Begin each day's study with this prayer or one of your own:

"Thou tellest my wanderings:
put thou my tears into thy bottle:
are they not in thy book?"

Psalm 56: 8 (KJV)

Thank you God that you care about and will acknowledge my grief for my child. You know all things. You know where grief has taken me and understand. Your love will be with me and my child forever.

Amen

Read John 18: 12-40

A detachment of Roman soldiers and Jewish officials has arrested Jesus. He was bound like a common criminal and brought before Annas, who was the father-in-law of Caiaphas, the high priest that year. Caiaphas was the one who had advised the Jews that it would be good if one man (Jesus) died for the people.

Peter and another disciple follow Jesus. They were frightened by what was happening. They feared their own arrest. Peter does exactly what Jesus said he would do. He denied knowing Jesus three times.

Mark 14: 72 (NIV)

Immediately the rooster crowed the second time. Then Peter remembered the word Jesus had spoken to him: "Before the rooster crows twice you will disown me three times." And he broke down and wept.

Jesus is taken before Pilate, the Roman governor. The Jewish officials wanted Jesus killed. Roman law prohibited the Jews from instituting a death penalty for a Roman citizen. Therefore, they trumped up a charge against Jesus that would be considered treason. They accused Jesus of claiming to be the king of the Jews. Caesar was king of the Jews and all other citizens of Rome.

Verses John 18: 33-34 (NIV) Please fill in the blanks:

Pilate then went back inside the palace, summoned Jesus and asked him, "Are you the _____ of the

223

_____?"

"Is that your _____ _____," Jesus asked, or did _____

_____ to you about me?

Pilate still wasn't understanding the trumped up charge against Jesus. What is it he has done? Obviously, Pilate questioned the validity of their charges. Yet, the size and anger of the crowd worried him enough to carry on.

Verses 36-37 (NIV) Please fill in the blanks:

Jesus said, "My kingdom is not of _____ _____. If it were, my servants would

_____ to prevent my arrest by the Jews. But my kingdom is from another place."

"You are a _____, then! said Pilate. Jesus answered, "You are _____

in saying I am a _____. In fact, for this reason I was born, and for this I came into the world,

to _____ to the _____. Everyone on the _____ of

_____ listens to me."

Jesus is a master at speaking the truth. The trouble with Pilate is that he didn't have eyes to see nor ears to hear the truth. He was blinded by the world's idea of truth.

Verse 38 (NIV) Please fill in the blank:

"What is _____?" Pilate asked. With this he went out again to the Jews and said, "I find no basis for a charge against him."

The Truth was standing in front of him and he couldn't see him.

Read John 19: 1-16

Pilate had just said that he found no basis to charge Jesus. Chapter 19 begins with Pilate's order to have Jesus flogged. Flogging was gruesome. The victim was bound to a whipping post and beaten on his front and back with a whip designed to inflict the maximum amount of pain. The lash was a long leather thong, studded at intervals with pellets of lead and sharpened pieces of bone. The idea was to shred the flesh and expose the internal organs. He was beaten beyond recognition. Pilate hoped this would suffice the crowd so that he could release this man he knew in his heart was innocent.

Isaiah 50: 6-7 (NIV)

> "I offered my back to those who beat me,
> my cheeks to those who pulled out my beard;
> I did not hide my face from mocking and spitting.
> Because the Sovereign Lord helps me,
> I will not be disgraced.
> Therefore have I set my face like flint,
> and I know I will not be put to shame."

Read Isaiah 52: 13-15

Verse 14 (NIV)

> "Just as there were many who were appalled at him—
> his appearance was so disfigured
> beyond that of any man
> and his form marred beyond human likeness—"

Read John 19: 16-27

Why? Why the mockery? Why the brutality? What had he done to merit such cruelty? Why was the crowd so thirsty for his blood? The answer is Evil, Satan in human form.

Jesus prayed that his followers would not fall into temptation. God has designed a new world with Jesus. He sent Jesus to lead the world by example to a world empowered with his love. Kingdom living on earth as it is in heaven is God's will. It was his will from before the foundation of the world.

Verses 25-26 (NIV) Please fill in the blanks:

Near the cross of Jesus stood his _____, his _____ _____,

Mary the wife of Clopas, and Mary Magdalene.

When Jesus saw _____ _____ there, and the disciple _____

_____ _____ standing nearby, he said to his mother, "_____

_____, here is your son." And to the disciple, "Here is your _____." From that time

on, this disciple took her into his home.

From the agony of the Cross, Jesus looked down at his mother and asked John to take care of her. Compassionately, he provided for his mother. Can you imagine the look of grief on her face? Can you feel her pain—a mother watching her son die?

John, the beloved disciple, was probably a boy or a very young man at this time. If that's true, he wouldn't have drawn much attention from the authorities. They wouldn't have seen him as a threat. Mary's sister was Salome. Salome was John's mother, making John and Jesus cousins.[16] It would make perfect sense for Jesus' mother to live with her sister and John.

Read John 19: 28-42

Once again, John, the eye witness, testifies that Jesus was the Messiah promised by the ancient prophets. Verse 36 tells us that these things happened so that the scripture would be fulfilled. "Not one of his bones will be broken,"

(Psalm 34: 20; Exodus 12: 46) and, as another scripture says, "They will look on the one they have pierced." (Psalm 22: 16; Zec 12: 10; Rev 1: 7) A prophesy was believed when it came true.

1. Do you believe that Jesus was the promised Messiah?

---

[16]*The Daily Study Bible Series; the Gospel of John, volume 2*, revised edition, by William Barclay, © 1975, by William Barclay, published by Westminister John Knox Press, Louisville, Kentucky, pgs. 256, 257

DAY 2: THE EMPTY TOMB

Opening Prayer:

"Thou tellest my wanderings:
put thou my tears into thy bottle:
are they not in thy book?"

                              Psalm 56: 8 (KJV)

Thank you God that you care about and will acknowledge my grief for my child. You know all things. You know where grief has taken me and understand. Your love will be with me and my child forever.

                                                            Amen

Read John 20: 1-9

Early on the first day of the week, while it was still dark, Mary Magdalene went to the tomb and saw that the stone had been removed from the entrance. So she came running to Simon Peter and the other disciple, the one Jesus loved, and said, "They have taken the Lord out of the tomb, and we don't know where they have put him!"

Verse 8 (NIV) Please fill in the blanks:

Finally the other disciple, who had reached the tomb first, also went inside. He _____ and

_____.

Read John 20: 10-18

Verses 11-12 (NIV) Please fill in the blanks:

But Mary stood outside the tomb crying. As she wept, she bent over to look into the tomb and saw

_____ _____ in white, seated where Jesus' body had been one at the head and one at

the foot.

Two angels were there where Mary expected Jesus to be. The linen cloths in which Jesus had been wrapped for burial were lying in folds as if he had escaped them. They weren't disheveled as if they had been taken off by someone but were lying in folds.

The angels asked Mary why she was crying.

Verse 15 (NIV)

"Woman," he said, "why are you crying? Who is it you are looking for?"

Mary thought it was the gardener talking to her. In her realm of thinking, who else could it be? She had witnessed the crucifixion first hand. She saw Jesus die. The furthest thing from her mind would be that Jesus was talking to her.

Verse 16 (NIV) Please fill in the blank:

Jesus said to her, "_____."

Through her tears she didn't recognize Jesus at first. Overcome with grief she had gone to the tomb. There she wept. Head bowed and inconsolable.

To Mary is given the glory of being the first to see the risen Christ. Jesus then sends her back to tell the others.

Verse 18 (NIV) Please fill in the blanks:

Mary Magdalene went to the disciples with the news: "I _____ _____ the

_____!"

Read John 20: 19-31

On the evening of that first day of the week, when the disciples were together, with the doors locked for fear of the Jews, Jesus came and stood among them and said, "Peace be with you!"

Verse 22 (NIV) Please fill in the blanks:

And with that he breathed on them and said, "Receive the _____ _____.

The disciples were overjoyed when they saw the Lord. Then Jesus did what he said he would do when he left them—he breathed the Holy Spirit into them. Faith is a gift from the Spirit.

Thomas is usually criticized by modern theologians. He is commonly referred to as doubting Thomas. However, Thomas wasn't present at that first meeting with Jesus and the disciples. He said that he wouldn't believe unless he saw the nail prints in Jesus' hands and put his finger in his pierced side.

Jesus honored his request and ***also gave Thomas the Holy Spirit***.

Galatians 5: 22-23 (NIV)

"But the fruit of the Spirit is love, joy, peace, patience, kindness, goodness, *faithfulness*, gentleness, and self-control. Against such things there is no control."

Notice that "fruit" is singular. When Jesus breathes the Holy Spirit into a person they receive all of the fruit of the Spirit. They come as a package deal.

Verses John 20: 28-29 (NIV) Please fill in the blanks:

Thomas said to him, "My Lord and my God!"

Then Jesus told him, "Because you have _____ me, you have _____;

_____ are those who have not _____ and yet have _____."

Would we have been any different than Thomas? The story of the life, death, and resurrection of Jesus is quite a story. The passion story would have been a tragic end to hope. Without the resurrection, evil would have had the last word. The last word was God's children proclaiming, "I have seen the Lord! He is risen!" With that is the victory of the Cross.

When our spiritual eyes have seen the Lord, we too, receive the fruit of the Spirit. Then our doubt becomes belief and belief becomes hope.

1. What do you believe about the life, death, and resurrection of Jesus? Have you seen the Lord?

DAY 3: JESUS APPEARS THE THIRD TIME

Opening Prayer:

"Thou tellest my wanderings:
put thou my tears into thy bottle:
are they not in thy book?"

Psalm 56: 8 (KJV)

Thank you God that you care about and will acknowledge my grief for my child. You know all things. You know where grief has taken me and understand. Your love will be with me and my child forever.

Amen

Read John 21: 1-14

Verse 4 (NIV) Please fill in the blanks:

Early in the morning, _____ stood on the shore, but the disciples did not _____ that it was_____.

Peter and the other disciples were fishing. Fishing was done at night at this period of time. Jesus was standing on the shore by the Sea of Tiberias.

Verse 5 (NIV) Please fill in the blanks:

He called out to them, "_____, haven't you any fish?"

Friends. How amazing is that? Jesus calls the fishermen friends. Jesus knows who they are but they don't recognize him yet. Remember it is early in the morning. Possibly it wasn't quite light yet. Again, the disciples weren't expecting Jesus to walk among them as their risen friend. It must have been exciting to say the least.

Verse 7 (NIV) Please fill in the blank:

Then the disciple whom Jesus loved said to Peter, "It is the _____!"

230

As soon as Simon Peter heard him say, "It is the Lord," he wrapped his outer garment around him (for he had taken it off) and jumped into the water.

1. What did Jesus ask his disciples to do in verses 12-14?

Jesus asked his disciples to come and eat breakfast with him. This was the third time that Jesus appeared to his disciples. One more time, Jesus appears to his disciples as confirmation that the resurrection was real. He was about to commission them to take his message to the world. Jesus had one last meal with them to insure that they knew that Jesus would be with them always.

Read John 21: 15-25

Verse 15 (NIV) Please fill in the blanks:

When they had finished eating, Jesus said to Simon Peter, "Simon son of John, do you _____

_____ _____ more than these?" "Yes Lord, he said, "you know that I love you." Jesus said, "Feed my lambs."

Jesus asked Peter the same question two more times. Could it be that he asked the same question three times—once for each time he denied him? Jesus was giving Peter a huge mission. He had told him (Matthew 16:18) that on Peter he would build the Church.

Matthew 16: 17-20 (NIV)

Jesus replied, "Blessed are you, Simon son of Jonah, for this was not revealed to you by man, but my Father in heaven. And I tell you that you are Peter, and on this rock I will build my church, and the gates of Hades will not overcome it. I will give you the keys of the kingdom of heaven; whatever you bind on earth will be bound in heaven, and whatever you loose on earth will be loosed in heaven." Then he warned his disciples not to tell anyone that he was the Christ.

Verses John 21: 18-19 (NIV) Please fill in the blanks:

"I tell you the _____, when you were younger you dressed yourself and went where you wanted; but when you are _____ you will _____ _____ _____ _____, and someone else will _____ you and _____ _____ where you do not _____ _____ _____."

Jesus said this to indicate the kind of _____ by which Peter would _____ _____. Then he said to him, "_____ _____!"

Jesus knew what was in store for Peter and the other disciples. They would face persecution even unto death. Jesus knew that Peter would have what it would take to follow his teaching and not cower in fear this time.

2. In verses 20 and 21, what does Peter ask Jesus?

What about John? Is he going to die for the cause, too?

Verse 22 (NIV) Please fill in the blanks:

Jesus answered, "If I want him to _____ _____ until I return, what is that to you? You must _____ _____."

Remember that it was John who Jesus gave the task of taking care of his mother.

John finishes his gospel by telling the reader that he testifies as an eye witness. He tells the reader that he knows the things he reveals are true because he was there. He saw them happen.

Then he tells us, Jesus did many other things as well. If every one of them were written down, I (John) suppose that even the whole world would not have room for the books that would be written.

John is an old man. He is exiled on the island of Patmos. He not only knew that he was dearly loved by Jesus, he also loved Jesus very much. He revered him and wanted the world to know how love changes the world and the heart of everyone who believes.

DAY 4: JOHN'S REVELATION

Opening Prayer:

"Thou tellest my wanderings:
put thou my tears into thy bottle:
are they not in thy book?"

Psalm 56: 8 (KJV)

Thank you God that you care about and will acknowledge my grief for my child. You know all things. You know where grief has taken me and understand. Your love will be with me and my child forever.

Amen

Read Revelation 1: 1- 3: 21 (It would be helpful to read the entire Book of Revelation if time permits)

Many scholars believe that John is the author of Revelation. John uses a lot of symbolism to tell his story. It would have been dangerous for John to speak clearly. He spoke in terms that Christians would understand but not necessarily the Roman authorities.

The other disciples including Paul had been martyred by this time. It makes sense that God would have given this revelation to John in his old age.

Chapter 1 begins by saying that this is the revelation of Jesus Christ, which God gave him to show his servants what soon must take place. He made it known by sending his angel to his servant John, who testifies to everything he saw—that is, the word of God and the testimony of Jesus Christ. Blessed is the one who reads the words of this prophesy, and blessed are those who hear it and take to heart what is written in it because the time is near.

Don't let the strange word pictures scare you. The Revelation is meant for comfort to bless the believer.

The Seven Churches

When used in scripture, seven is a complete number. There were more than seven churches. The revelation is intended to include the Church of Christian believers.

There is a formula that Jesus uses for each church. He says that he has certain things for the church and certain things against the church. Then he tells the church what they need to do make things right with God. The final thing he tells the church is that if they overcome he promises them something.

We won't have time to fill in the entire formula for each church. However, we are going to learn what Jesus promises to him who overcomes.

Ephesus—Revelation 2: 1-7

1. What is the promise for him who overcomes in verse 7?

"He who has an ear, let him hear what the Spirit says to the churches. To him who overcomes, I will give the right to eat from the tree of life, which is in the paradise of God.

Smyrna—Revelation 2: 8-11

2. What is the promise for him who overcomes in verse 11?

"He who has an ear, let him hear what the Spirit says to the churches. He who overcomes will not be hurt at all by the second death."

Pergamum—Revelation 2: 12-17

3. What is the promise for him who overcomes in verse 17?

"He who has an ear, let him hear what the Spirit says to the churches. To him who overcomes, I will give some hidden manna. I will also give him a white stone with a new name written on it, known only to him who receives it."

Thyatira—Revelation 2: 18-29

4. What is the promise for him who overcomes in verses 26-29?

"To him who overcomes and does my will to the end, I will give authority over the nations—he will rule them with an iron scepter; he will dash them to pieces like pottery—(Isaiah 30: 14) just as I have received authority from my Father. I will also give him the morning star (Nu 24:17). He who has an ear, let him hear what the Spirit says to the churches.

Sardis—Revelation 3: 1-6

5. What is the promise for him who overcomes in verses 5-6?

"He who overcomes will, like them, be dressed in white. I will never blot out his name from the book of life, but will acknowledge his name before my Father and his angels. He who has an ear, let him hear what the Spirit says to the churches.

Philadelphia—Revelation 3: 7-13

6. What is the promise for him who overcomes in verse 12-13?

"Him who overcomes I will make a pillar in the temple of my God. Never again will he leave it. I will write on him the name of my God and the name of the city of my God; and I will also write on him my new name. He who has an ear, let him hear what the Spirit says to the churches."

Laodicea—Revelation 3: 14-22

7. What is the promise for him who overcomes in verses 21-22?

"To him who overcomes, I will give the right to sit with me on my throne, just as I overcame and sat down with my Father on his throne. He who has an ear, let him hear what the Spirit says to the churches."

8. Do you believe these same promises are available for today's believer? Do you believe that you are among those in the Church who have overcome?

DAY 5: THE NEW JERUSALEM

Opening Prayer:

"Thou tellest my wanderings:
put thou my tears into thy bottle:
are they not in thy book?"

Psalm 56: 8 (KJV)

Thank you God that you care about and will acknowledge my grief for my child. You know all things. You know where grief has taken me and understand. Your love will be with me and my child forever.

Amen

Read Revelation 21: 1-22: 21

Verses 21: 1-4 (NIV) Please fill in the blanks:

"Then I saw a new heaven and a new earth, for the first heaven and the first earth had passed away, and there

was _____ _____ any _____. I saw the Holy City, the _____

_____, coming down out of heaven from _____, prepared as a bride

beautifully dressed for her husband. And I heard a loud voice from the throne saying, "Now the dwelling of God

is _____ _____, and he will _____ with them. They will be

_____ people, and _____ _____ will be with them and be their God.

He will _____ _____ _____ from their eyes. There will be no

more _____ or _____ or _____ or _____,

for the old order of things has passed away.

The believer is promised fellowship with God. God will make his dwelling among his people. They will be his people and he will be their God, a promise throughout the Old Testament.

The first thing mentioned about the new Jerusalem is that the sea will be no more. No more chaos, storms, or dangers.

239

He will wipe every tear from their eyes. God will acknowledge the suffering of his children. He promises no more death or mourning.

Isaiah 25: 8 (NIV)

"he will swallow up death forever.
The Sovereign Lord will wipe away the tears from all faces;
he will remove the disgrace of his people from all the earth.
The Lord has spoken."

Revelation 7: 17 (NIV)

"For the Lamb at the center of the
throne will be their shepherd;
he will lead them to springs of living water.
And God will wipe away every tear from their eyes."

Psalm 56:8 (NIV)

"Record my lament;
list my tears on your scroll—
are they not in your record?"

Psalm 56: 8 (KJV)

"Thou tellest my wanderings:
put thou my tears into thy bottle:
are they not in thy book?"

1. Does it mean anything to you that God puts your tears in a bottle to acknowledge when you get to paradise?

Verse 21: 21 (NIV) Please fill in the blanks:

The twelve gates were _____ _____, each gate made of a

_____ _____. The great street of the city was of pure gold, like transparent

glass.

The city itself was of pure gold, so pure that it seemed like transparent glass. The city had twelve foundation stones which were layers of precious stones. The most wonderfully illuminating of the precious stones usage was the twelve gates. Each gate was one pearl. In the ancient world, pearls were the most valued. Gates of pearl are a symbol of unimaginable beauty and unassessable riches.[17]

Knowing that pearls are made by the oyster and are constructed out of an irritant and pain adds a new dimension to the beauty of this picture. Twelve huge, precious and priceless pearls born from adversity guard the gates of the paradise of God.

The River of Life: Revelation 22: 1-6 (NIV)

Then the angel showed me the river of the water of life, as clear as crystal, flowing from the throne of God and of the Lamb down the middle of the great street of the city. On each side of the river stood the tree of life, bearing twelve crops of fruit, yielding its fruit every month. And the leaves of the tree are for the healing of the nations. No longer will there be any curse. The throne of God and of the Lamb will be in the city, and his servants will serve him. They will see his face, and his name will be on their foreheads. There will be no more night. They will not need the light of a lamp or the light of the sun, for the Lord God will give them light. And they will reign for ever and ever.

Verse 7 (NIV) Please fill in the blanks:

"Behold, I am _____ _____! _____ is he who keeps

the words of the prophecy in this book."

Praise God! Amen.

[17]*The Daily Study Bible Series, the Revelation of John, Volume 2, Revised Edition*, by William Barclay, © 1976 William Barclay, published by The Westminister Press, Philadelphia, Pennsylvania.

My Name Is Joy — by Elaine

I was leading a Bible study by Beth Moore titled *Beloved Disciple.* From that study, I learned of the formula for each of the seven churches. As I was preparing to teach the lesson for the week, I was filling in the formula for each church as instructed by Beth for homework. I came to the church at Pergamum and the part where I was to fill in "to him who overcomes." God whispered to me that he was giving me a new name. I would recognize this name as it would be written on a white stone.

For a few weeks I searched out white stones with excitement and wonder. Abraham was changed from Abram and Sarah from Sarai (Genesis 17: 5, 15). What's close to Elaine I wondered? After a few weeks, I thought that I must have not heard from God after all because I hadn't seen a white stone with a name on it.

We were moving again in a couple of months. We already knew where we moving to and I was devastated. As United Methodists, we agree to go where we are sent by the bishop. We were moving to Southwest Missouri only four miles from Arkansas. My support group that I had developed after losing Craig would be gone. I would no longer be able to attend TCF group meetings that had helped me so much. At these meetings, I could be Elaine and not the pastor's wife. They weren't shocked when I doubted my faith. I became very close to one friend in particular. I could talk to her about anything including my faith struggle.

Even more important to me in my healing, was the fact that my other children were only about an hour from me. I had a new grandson and I wanted to see him often. We were moving three hours away from them. My sisters and brothers as well as my mom were close enough that I saw them often. David's family was even closer. And Craig was buried in a cemetery only twenty minutes from our home. It would be five hours to visit the cemetery. I told David, "I can't go." David seriously considered leaving the ministry or leaving me behind with the kids. I needed him too much for that to happen. So, we were moving.

Every year we have an annual conference where all of the Missouri pastors and a lay delegate from each charge meet to vote on the issues concerning the church. Basically it's a business meeting. I liked to go because there is usually awesome worship and it's a chance to get away with David and see other friends in ministry whom we don't see very often.

This year I went mostly to lick my wounds of moving. I stayed in the motel room most of the time feeling very sad. However, I did attend worship because I knew that is what I needed. We were singing a worship song with the words displayed from a PowerPoint slide presentation on a huge screen in the front of the room. At one point, in the middle of the song a white rock appeared in the background with a word written on it. The word had nothing to do with the song we were singing but my heart skipped a beat. I looked over at David and he saw it, too. Then I talked myself out of my new name because the rock was really kind of gray and not white. Then it appeared again and this time the stone was *white*. I started to cry with every emotion. I was sad, excited, happy, mad, relieved, affirmed, and confused. God expected "Joy" from me after losing Craig and having to move so far from my kids.

I always know something is from God when I would never have thought of it on my own. I certainly wouldn't have given myself the name Joy at that time of my life. In fact, it made me mad. I have since learned to cherish it. I now realize that it is an affirmation of the time I've spent finding my way back to the arms of my loving Father and learning to live my life in joy.

The joy of the Lord is my strength (Nehemiah 8: 10). Like Job, I have seen the face of God which means that my spiritual eyes have seen the truth about God as revealed to me by the Holy Spirit in his Word.

Even now, I miss Craig with every breath I take. I will love him until I take my last breath and then on into eternity. My God who tells the caterpillar it's time to spin a cocoon around itself and transform from a worm crawling on the ground to the freedom of flight as a beautiful butterfly has taken my shattered heart and given it wings again. I'll never be over "it" but I've learned to take Craig forward with me. My precious son is with me with every step I take.

I love you, Craig.

•••

Springtime

The seed of love planted in my womb,
still grows in the fertile soil of my heart.
Nourished by memories and warm Sonshine,
Spring's promise giving it a brand new start.

It took some time to plow the rocky ground.
Weed and bug control has been quite the problem.
But, watered by cloudbursts of huge teardrops,
it blossomed from deeper root and stronger stem.

Its color has become more intense and vivid.
Its fragrance more pleasant and sweet.
Its flower's petal is soft and rich like velvet.
Its song made vibrant by sounds of past defeat.

A heart that once felt like barren wasteland,
yearning for love's fresh air to breathe free.
Graceful butterflies now feed on its nectar,
giving it wings to be all it was meant to be.

In loving memory of Craig,
Feb. 13, 1982—June 28, 2000
written by Elaine Howlett
April 13, 2002

All Things Become New — by David

During my personal observations at the end of week 2, I mentioned how a certain man helped me with my grief. In addition to the advice mentioned earlier, this same mentor shared more solid words with me. Like me, he is a bereaved father and his words I still remember clearly. He said that my life would always be different than it was before Craig's death. My life, he said, would be lived in a narrower band than before. The good news, he said, is that there would come a time when I would have more good days between the bad days. The not so good news is that my good days will never be as good as they were before.

Somewhere in all the confusion of those first several years, I had enough sense to listen to this man and follow his mentoring. I realized that I didn't know how to chart my own course in this new and strange world which I found myself. I have also found his insight about the narrowing of my world to be very true.

I don't cry as much now as I did. My thoughts of Craig are more on his life and not exclusively about his death. I still miss him. I am not ambushed by sights and sounds as much as earlier in the grief process. There are still times when I fight depression. I have attended Compassionate Friends meetings with two different chapters and have found much love and support in them. I still process information through the experience of my grief. On the whole, my life is as normal as my new normal will ever allow it to be.

But there is also the other side. The side where lows are not as low, but the highs are not as high either. Anniversaries and birthday celebrations carry with them a sadness that I try hard not to share with others. Holidays can be stressful. Listening to other parents complain about the normal unruly behavior of their children drives me to distraction. I want to say to them, "At least you can hold, touch, see, and listen to your child." Listening to unexamined but sincerely held theology of others can be hard to accept.

The biggest difference in my spiritual life now compared to those days after Craig's death is the return of hope. Over the last decade as I reflect on events and people who have graced my life with their presence, I see how God has been with me from the beginning in my spiritual journey. I don't have all the answers figured out, and while I don't think it is unfaithful to ask the questions and not settle for cheap explanations, I know that much of the mystery is simply beyond my understanding in this world.

The reconstruction of my faith has not been easy. It has been through God's providential care and the help of many other hurting parents, that I have been able to find hope again. It has been through the unconditional love of Elaine, our kids, and grandkids that I have the strength to move forward. Healing has come about through hard work and stubbornness.

I find it interesting that at this place in my life, I find comfort in two different Bible books that most people find strange and baffling. I have mentioned earlier how the Old Testament Book of Job has become a source of help. In the New Testament I have found certain parts of Revelation to be unexpected wells of support.

Not having the pie-in-the-sky view that so many people have of Revelation, I am not sitting around doing nothing and waiting for the end of time to arrive. I do look forward to a place and time when all things will become new and where there will be no more sickness, accidents, death, or separation. I look forward to the time when God's reign becomes concrete reality. However, I took comfort in these verses before June of 2000.

I look forward to the time and place where all the hurts and enemies of life will be no more. My heart jumps for joy when I read the words of Revelation 7: 17.

> "For the Lamb at the center of the
> throne will be their shepherd;
> he will lead them to springs of living water,
> And God will wipe away every tear
> from their eyes."

What an affirmation for hope-filled living this verse gives to a seeking heart. I don't have all things figured out and my spiritual life is still growing but I know that the truths expressed in Revelation 21: 3-4 are true.

> "See the home of God is among mortals.
> He will dwell with them; they will be his people,
> and God himself will be with them;
> He will wipe every tear from their eyes.
> Death will be no more;
> mourning and crying and pain will be no more,
> for the first things have passed away."

BIBLIOGRAPHY

Barclay, William. (1976). The Gospel of John volumes 1 & 2. The daily Bible study series revised edition. Philadelphia, PA: The Westminster Press.

Barclay, William. (1975). The Gospel of Luke. The daily Bible study series revised edition. Louisville, KY: Westminster John Knox Press.

Barclay, William. (1976). The Revelation of John volumes 1 & 2. The daily Bible study series revised edition. Philadelphia, PA: The Westminster Press.

Gibson, John C. L. (1985). Job. Louisville, KY: Westminster John Knox Press.

Goodrick, Edward W. and John R. Kohlenberger III. (1999). The Strongest NIV Exhaustive Concordance. Grand Rapids, MI: Zondervan.

International Bible Society. (1984). Holy Bible: New International Version. Grand Rapids: Zondervan Publishing House.

Knight, George A.F. (1983). Psalms volumes 1 & 2. The daily study Bible (old testament). Louisville, KY: Westminster John Knox Press.

Meeks, Blair Gilmer. (2002). Standing in the Circle of Grief. Nashville, TN: Abingdon Press.

The Message. Copyright © by Eugene H. Peterson, 1993, 1994, 1995, 1996, 2000, 2001, 2002. NavPress Publishing Group.

Moore, Beth. (2002). Beloved Disciple. The Life and Ministry of John. Nashville, TN: Life Way Press.

Sheppy, Paul. (2003). In Sure and Certain Hope. Nashville: Abingdon Press.

Smith, Harold Ivan (1982). Alive Now, September/October.

Strong, James. (1986). Strong's Exhaustive Concordance of the Bible. Nashville, TN; Abingdon Press.

TO ORDER
"LAZARUS, COME OUT!"

Through Centering Corporation
Grief Illustrated Press

www.centering.org
www.griefillustratedpress.org

Phone: 866-218-0101
Or 402-553-1200
Fax: 402-53-0507

Through the Authors
www.spiritualgrief.com

9